# Kissing Lions

By Daniel E. Lemke

15 months, 12,608-mile bicycle tour skirting the perimeter of America dedicated to raising awareness about domestic Sex Trafficking.

For those who
have been sexually
abused and need
to know what real
love is in Jesus
Christ.

ISBN Number: 978-1-5488-4070-9

Cover design by Allison Blake Photography

Edited by Blake Atwood Writing Solutions LLC.

# Contents

# Forward

My initial experience with Daniel was working in different departments in a retail store which sells mainly outdoor-themed products. We served many families, so it was not uncommon for those working in different departments to interact. A family was looking for snow sports helmets for their children and that's when I witnessed Daniels gentle caring side when, while speaking softly and lowering himself to her level, guided a 5-year old girl through the fitting process. I've seen this behavior in very few young men in their early 20s. This drew my attention to this unique guy.

I learned of Bike Through Traffic by reading a poster in the store breakroom for a concert to raise support for the upcoming trek. After attending the concert which included Daniel speaking about the trek and sex trafficking, I knew being involved in this effort was something I had to do. I was shocked and disgusted while listening to the stories of young girls and boys who were enslaved and one in particular of how a father had pimped out is 11 year old daughter to his friends and business clients. Daniel's passion about ending sex trafficking was and is infectious.

After talking to Daniel and learning more about his support team, I volunteered to assist him in editing his blogs and partnering with him to create a monthly newsletter. We also talked about writing a book based upon his trek and those he encountered along the journey. You're about to experience the result of what began during that conversation in March of 2015. Additionally, I committed to commuting back and forth to work by bicycle as many days as possible to support Daniel so he would never feel as though he was riding alone. This ignited a passion for cycling that continues to be part of my life.

Listening to Daniel recount stories during his trek, some of which you will read within these pages, at times brought me to tears and other times filled me with anger. His struggles and wrestling with the journey in front of him were very real to me, as my life has taken many turns, which had me questioning if God really cared about me. The short answer is YES! God not only cares for Daniel and I, but He loves you with a love that no human being could come close to duplicating.

There were many times when Daniel spoke of loneliness and desperately desiring company during the grind of day after day, mile after mile that I wanted to join him physically, not just through prayer, text messages, and phone conversations. This finally happened on June 30, 2016 when we met at the west gate of Rocky Mountain National Park (RMNP) to ride Trail Ridge Road together (44 miles, climbing over 4,000 ft. to 12,183 ft. [3,713 m]) and July 2, 2016 when we rode the final leg of Daniel's trek and his return to his hometown of Loveland, CO. His polite refusal to off load 100 pounds of gear into my empty car trunk (I was shuttled to the park entrance) speaks to his integrity and to finishing as he started. His joyful and uninhibited celebration upon passing through the East gate of RMNP and celebrating with him for about 1.5 miles is a memory which I will cherish. His passion for life and the lives of others is palpable.

As you read the words that follow, know that this young man who left at age 22 was much different from the man who finished what he began so many months and miles after he started. His life has changed physically, mentally, emotionally and spiritually. Although the book recounts the trek and cycling, the true focus is what Daniel remains passionate about, ending sex trafficking and rescuing those who are slaves. I encourage you to ponder while reading and ask yourself how you may assist in either becoming involved in the fight against sex trafficking or supporting those who are in the battle.

Daniel is the real deal and I've met with him several times as he's returned to Colorado from California where the next phase of his battling sex trafficking and caring for ex slaves continues. I'm honored to count Daniel as a friend and a brother.

Mike Woeckener
Pierce, Colorado
Joshua 1:9

# Intro

In this book are stories of my encounters during a fifteen-month bicycle tour I did to raise awareness about sex trafficking in the United States that I called, "Bike Through Traffic".

I've gotten to sleep in homes with pimps, johns, Hell's Angels, Skinheads, Banditos, co-producers of porn, victims of sex trafficking, drug dealers, those freshly out of jail, the poor, the extremely wealthy, the abused, neglected, mistreated, unloved, those in meth houses, those in recovery houses, and those in homeless shelters. I've even had bears and alligators greet me in my tent or hammock.

I shared the gospel with atheists, Satanists, Hindus, Buddhists, Muslims, and new-age free spirits. I biked through every single terrain imaginable and in about every weather possible. I experienced more heat exhaustion than I can count. I was put in the hospital for hypothermia. I was sleep deprived to the point of hallucination. I biked sixty to eighty miles in the blistering heat and pouring rain. I ran out of food and water plenty of times. I have been chased by enough animals to start my own zoo.

I spoke about sex trafficking and pornography in every major church denomination, whether it was to a full congregation, a small group, or a youth group. I was kicked out of churches and told that what I was doing wasn't biblical. I spoke in bars, concert halls, festivals, and cafes. I educated kids of all ages in the public school system from elementary to high school and spoke in lecture halls at many universities.

I sat down with politicians and judges. I taught law enforcement and firefighters what to look for when they may be in a situation to help a victim of sex trafficking and to arrest the right people. I listened to survivors' stories and sat down with other abolitionists. I discussed plans of action with CEOs of big corporations that they've implemented in their companies. I helped established educational programs in universities so students can learn what to look out for.

I have been persecuted, beat down, and defeated. But I've also been lifted up, victorious, and blessed beyond measure. That was my life for fifteen months.

I wrote this book for the general public and to those who know that sex trafficking is wrong, wants to change it, and yet may not know how.

The language I use in this book is written from my point of view as an abolitionist, and a Christian with love for everyone no matter their background.

Just because my love for Jesus Christ is prevalent in this book, please go into it with and open mind understanding that we are all in this together and should be fighting sex trafficking as one.

On April 19, 2015 I left my home in Colorado to circumnavigate the United States for fifteen months: a total of 12,608 miles. My purpose was to raise awareness about sex trafficking in America. I choose to use a bicycle as a tool, getting me into place I wouldn't have if I were in a car, and as an attention grabber.

The opening chapter starts in the middle of my tour in Atlanta Georgia. This moment in my life was very pivotal and gives the reader a good understanding of the thoughts and circumstances I endured throughout my tour. By chapter two the reader learns about my past and what led me to ride a bicycle to fight sex trafficking. The chapters that follow after are real life experiences and from my point of view. Also placed into the book are experts from my personal journal that I wrote in correspondence to a particular event.

A short disclaimer, I do use a few profanities, and some very graphic stories. These stories are real, and to help press the issues the wording I use is simply how it is. Also many of the names have been changed to protect the identity of said person.

*Sophia on the Katy Trail in Missouri*

# Totally Deflated

*Today I cried like I have never cried before. This was not a light drizzle that one brushes off their cheek. I am talking full-blown monsoon gushing out of every possible hole in my head with snot bubbling and my mind only on one thing: "Why?"*

~Daniel Lemke (journal entry)

Day 195 – Georgia

## October 30, 2015

Six months into my fifteen-month Bike Through Traffic tour of the U.S., the full weight of its twelve thousand miles pressed down on me like a napping elephant. I'd been ridiculed by major national media companies, torn down by the Christian church, and had experienced enough dangerous situations for a lifetime.

Even worse, I felt totally alone. Maybe it was poor planning on my part to do a solo bike tour around the states, but after six months of literal ups and downs giving way to incredible highs and lows within my spiritual life, I knew I couldn't give up.

Or could I?

I was emotionally beaten, physically drained, and spiritually empty. I longed to give up. I hated figuring out ways to entertain my mind for five to eight hours a day while biking. Insanity settled in and nestled itself into the crevices of my mind. I hated the thought of having to get on my bicycle one more time. No one seemed to understand what I endured on a daily basis to fight for the victims of sex trafficking. I was done.

In fact, I was so done that I had no desire to keep living.

## The Bottom of the Valley

At that point, I hadn't even made it to the halfway mark of the tour's full fifteen months. Fundraising and speaking engagements at churches were nowhere close to what I had hoped they would be. I'd been struggling to find places to sleep. I felt as alone as I'd ever felt, like the six months of my solo bicycle tour had accumulated depression with every push of the pedal. I was a tightly wound emotional coil whose pent-up sadness was soon to be released.

Then grace intervened in a form it's often taken in my life. At the lowest point of my trip, it just so happened that my mom came to Atlanta to attend a conference and visit me. Maybe moms have a secret way of knowing when their kids are in trouble, or maybe it's that God knows when to send moms in to do the work that only moms can do.

We spent a busy week together visiting tourist traps, museums, and watching movies. I spoke at several men's conferences and with local law enforcement about domestic child sex trafficking. It was a good week. But with as many miles as I'd ridden by then, I knew that the tallest peaks always gave way to the lowest valleys.

In a rented Ford F-150 truck that we had for the week, loaded with my bicycle and all of my gear, I dropped my mom off at the airport for her flight home. As I drove to return the rental, Passion's song "Even So Come" played on the radio. The chorus burst the dam of my long-held tear ducts. I felt as if God were reminding me, "Yes, you're alone, but have hope. You're getting ready for what's *next*." I cried so much that I missed my turn.

As I was filtered back onto the interstate, I considered driving all the way from Atlanta back to my home in Colorado—back to the life I once knew, back to my mom and my family, and back to friends. I reasoned with myself, *All of your gear is already stowed! It'd be so easy. Just keep driving. You've done well. Nothing to be ashamed of. Everybody will understand.*

I thought about what I would tell my friends, family, and other supporters who had been so encouraging when I'd first started the tour:

> *"The spiritual attacks are un-freaking-real. Have you seen the ridiculous and rude comments on my social media feeds? Did you know that my website got hacked and turned into a pro-pornography site?*
>
> *I feel really, really alone out there. Just imagine having to find someplace to stay each night and your new host has no idea what you've been through that day or the hundreds of days before that.*
>
> *The spiritual battles of my ride are real and intense. The enemy constantly tells me I am no good and I'm not doing a single thing right.*

17

Then I thought, *Yeah, that's a great way to say thanks. Maybe I should tone it down a bit.*

Even when I thought about how hard it would be to explain the reason I'd quit, the prospect of going home didn't look so bad. But God, as so often happens, had other plans.

## I'm Not Done!

The exit ramp for the rental company was fast approaching. My mind raced between exiting and giving up on this ridiculous idea God had implanted within me and just heading home. I firmly determined to stay the course: straight on till morning till I crossed the Colorado border.

But then, BLAM!

*Did I just hit a dragon?*

No more than a hundred yards from the drop-off location, through a mess of tears and confusion, I realized my front passenger tire had blown. The truck yelped and wobbled as it wrestled against itself. I gripped the steering wheel and coaxed it off the interstate, right onto the rental company's entryway.

Then, at that moment, God yelled at me: "I'm not done with you yet!"

I'm sure I must have laughed at that moment because God usually gives me more subtle signs.

An employee ran up to my now-defunct truck, wholly unaware of the emotional, hysterical, weeping, wreck she was about to encounter.

I shouted, "What do you want?"

18

Caught off guard by my yelling, she jumped back.

I pointed to my right front tire. She nodded her head. "I see. We'll take care of it." Then she motioned me to move forward because I was blocking their entry. I got out of the truck and stood in front of the rental facility. Tears, of which I seemed to have an endless supply that day, flowed freely once again. I told Christ, "This tour is no longer mine. You need to take the driver's seat, uh, handlebars. Just, Jesus, you know, take the wheel."

I slowly pulled my gear from the truck and got back on my saddle. I was a red-faced, emotionally drained, occasionally weepy solo bike rider fighting for the cause of the victims of sex trafficking. I was going to finish what God had told me to do.

Ironically enough, as if God weren't done having enough fun with me on that particular day, it was Halloween. Most people thought my biking outfit was my costume, even to the point where they'd make comments as I'd pass them by:

"Is that Lance Armstrong?"

"Great costume, you look like the real thing."

"Lookin' good, biker man!"

If they only knew.

## The Only Constant

With boring mile after mile to myself, I had plenty of time to ruminate and pray about why I'd come so close to giving up when I'd already put in six months of good work.

I was desperately lonely and hadn't wanted to admit it.

Realizing how deeply I needed to talk to someone who knew me well, I called my best friend. Of course, I had to leave a message. All I remember saying—through more tears—was, "I am so alone."

But how could I be so alone when I was constantly engaging and influencing people's life? I lacked the one thing we need to keep loneliness at bay: consistency. During the tour, every single day was filled with new people, new cities, new houses, new food, and wildly varying experiences. Change was the only constant on my daily schedule.

I'd convinced myself that I was completely alone and no one understood the kinds of daily sacrifices I was making to see this tour through to the end. I railed against people who tried to relate. I used that angry teenager standby excuse, "You don't know how I feel!"

As those thoughts ran through my mind, I considered my spiritual mindset when I'd first begun the tour. I'd placed Jesus on the nonexistent back seat of my bicycle and had effectively told him, "Yo, you can tag along with me if you'd like."

But after Atlanta, and everything that had led me to Atlanta, I was reminded that I couldn't have done any of it—and wouldn't be able to keep pedaling and preaching—without Jesus.

So, on my way to my next stop, I asked him, "Hey, Jesus? You mind if I tag along with you?"

# The Life of Lemke

*"God doesn't give us good days, He doesn't give us bad days, He gives us days that makes us who we are."*
~ Pastor Mike Williams

I was born and raised with my two brothers in the mountains of Colorado by a single mother of three boys. I attended my church's youth group in high school, but for me it was a place to hang out with friends and chase cute girls. At the time, I felt popular and carried a huge ego. I didn't think I needed Christ because my life was going how I wanted it to—or so I thought. Along with youth group and churches, I also grew up going to a Christian camp called Covenant Heights in Estes Park, Colorado. I always spent spare weekends there because it was yet another escape, and there was always a plethora of new girls to chase.

For me, Jesus Christ sat on the long-simmering back burner of an almost forgotten stove—until he lit up my heart near a campfire.

I don't remember applying to work as a camp counselor at Covenant Heights, but I received a call four months before the end of my freshman year of college saying that I'd gotten the job. Three weeks before camp began, I threw a party that lasted three weeks. It was a last-ditch effort to be the popular and cool guy I wanted to be.

As my best friend Elijah drove me up to camp I remember asking Jesus, *Why the heck do you have someone like me working up here with children?* The response I got was, *You'll see.*

With those words I arrived at camp, my mind somewhere else and my body likely still reeking of alcohol.

After having met the other staffers on the first day, a group of my colleagues decided to have a worship night the following evening. They invited everyone to come. As we gathered around the roaring campfire under the stars that painted the sky better than Van Gogh, and a half-moon that silhouetted the fourteen-thousand-foot mountains that fully encircled our surroundings. I was brought to my knees.

The best way I can describe what happened next was a Jesus dropkick to the face.

As I was lying on the ground, I felt a hand grab me and hoist me up. However, all of my friends were in a circle around the fire. I was outside of the circle just far enough away to be alone yet still hear the music resonating off of Twin Sisters Peaks. At that moment, I distinctly heard Jesus tell me, *You are mine now. I love you, but I am not fond of the life you are living. If you are ready, I want you to follow me now.*

Tears welled up in my eyes. All I could say was yes.

The radical part about this encounter was from that point on I had no desire to smoke, or get drunk. I solely desired to chase Christ and make Him my addiction.

## The Collegian

During those two life-changing months that summer, I bonded with a few other staffers like myself. They told me of a phenomenal university in Chicago called North Park University. They said I should come to school with them, and I jumped on board. When the summer ended, I left for Chicago to become a North Park student of Biblical and Theological studies.

I didn't have many scholarships, so I worked two jobs while going to school full-time. These jobs were in an area of Chicago called Andersonville, which is also referred to as "Boystown" because of the large gay community that resides there. I worked at a bar and a gym on the same block, so I developed friendships with many people because I'd see them at both places.

After a few months in Chicago, I struggled with why I was even there in the first place. One day, I yelled at God and asked him to show me a sign. I kept asking for weeks. Did I expect an answer? Maybe, but not in the way it came. As I was walking back to my apartment, I saw the reflection of an Ichthus on an apartment building—but that wasn't the real sign. A couple of weeks later, I was fired for the first time in my life.

My boss at the bar didn't like how much I talked to the customers about Jesus. I couldn't help it! I was a Biblical and Theological major and Christ came up all the time. Clients would ask me what I was doing in Chicago and so, I'd tell them:

"I'm studying Christ".

The best part about those jobs were that they opened some amazing doors. On many occasions, the customers would open up to me at the bar and pour out their beliefs. They'd share why they didn't like Christ, which then allowed me to share my testimony.

I'd often hear, "You're different," along with the occasional man hitting on me because he thought I was good-looking. I didn't mind because I knew I needed to show them love and do exactly what Jesus would have done as well.

Getting fired from the bar allowed me to spend more time at the gym, where I was supposed to talk with the clients. Not necessarily about Christ, but like I said, Jesus came up in my casual conversations because he had become my life.

## The Dropout

At the gym, we had a client who was a police officer; he would sometimes talk with me about a case he'd just closed or what his line of work entailed. One day, he told me about an older case that had happened three stores down from the gym. A lady who ran a nail salon had been selling children to strangers in exchange for sex. He told me that it had taken the police force two-and-a-half years to convict her. Then she was only in jail for four months.

After hearing this, I freaked out because I knew this was not ok. Exploiting someone else, especially a child, for personal gain is wrong. My protective spirit burst forth. I was furious and couldn't think of anything else other than, *How could this be, and why is this happening?*

I began conducting my own research and discovered that an overwhelming amount of sex-trafficking cases exist just in the United States alone. For the next several weeks, I went around to my coworkers, friends, teachers, and pastors to see if they knew about this. Many of them had no idea that it even existed, let alone that it happened in our own backyards. It wasn't just happening in big cities either. A lot of the time, sex trafficking was occurring in cities I'd never heard of. Its locations looked like a cell phone coverage map, with a majority of America covered in known cases of domestic sex trafficking. Also, not one gender, ethnicity, or background, whether rich or poor, was trafficking or being trafficked more than another.

Sex trafficking was an epidemic without borders. It was a monster with too many heads that could shape-shift at the same time. I had no idea what I could even do about it or where to begin. This problem was so huge and over my head, but I felt the call to go and defend "*the least of these*" (Matt 25), to take a stand for these children who were being robbed of their innocence on a daily basis. I wanted to be able to give these kids the lives they deserved rather than the lives they'd been given.

Shortly after this revelation, my buddy from Covenant Heights, Truyn Mosher, called me up with a grand idea to bicycle across America after we graduated, just for the heck of it. I'd always wanted to do that just to say I'd done it. I knew that if I were to do so, I'd certainly talk to people along the way. As I sat on that thought, I asked myself,

*What the heck would I talk to people about?*

*I could talk to them about Christ, of course, but I need something else to draw them in. I have cousins in Africa, and I know that there's a huge water crisis there. I also know about the Invisible Children, the kids who were abducted at a young age and forced into the rebel army.*[1]

As I pondered all the problems of the world, the answer screeched my mental brakes.

*Duh, Daniel! Talk to people about the issue of domestic sex trafficking.*

Later sat down with my guidance counselor at North Park and told her my thoughts. I relayed that I was going to drop out of school to ride my bicycle across the United States to raise awareness about domestic sex trafficking.

As we sat in the grass eating sandwiches, she looked at me and said, "I wouldn't suggest that you drop out, but if this is where you feel called, then let me help you."

I finished the semester strong with all A's and only a couple thousand dollars in debt. I was determined to get out of debt before I left for my tour and I also knew that I'd need time to plan and organize. I left North Park in December of 2013 and knew I'd begin my tour in April of 2015. That'd give me just over a year to plan my fifteen-month, twelve-thousand-mile bicycle tour skirting the perimeter of the United States.

When I left school, I moved to Cheyenne, Wyoming to live with my best friends, Caleb and his wife, Aishlinn. I worked for a tax attorney and started planning my tour.

However, when I left school I originally thought my tour wouldn't be that long. Initially, I'd planned a route from Colorado to Florida, then to Virginia, and back. But God, as usual, had other plans for me.

## The Nonprofit Cyclist

At the time, my mom was reading *The Circle Maker* by Pastor Mark Batterson. He talks about encasing your house, neighborhood, city, and workplace in prayer by walking around it and praying. Long story short: God told me to bicycle around the United States and encase it in prayer. I got on my computer and looked up the top twenty-five cities with the most sex-trafficking cases. I mapped my route through every one of those cities. My tour quickly expanded to the four "corners" of America, starting in my home state of Colorado.

I knew I'd need to start a nonprofit, but I wasn't sure how to go about it. I leveraged my business background and researched all that I could on how to start and maintain a nonprofit entity. I spent a little over a month getting all the paperwork together and submitted. If you've never started a business, let me tell you, it is not easy.

Nonprofits are difficult to start and can cost an arm and a leg. However, when God is your sponsor, incredible things happen. The average time to hear back from the IRS on whether or not you'll receive tax-exempt status is three to eleven months. Back then, I was working with a local anti-sex-trafficking organization and they'd been waiting for a year-and-a-half. I didn't think I'd have my nonprofit status until well into my tour.

I submitted my request during tax season and was ready to start working on other things while it was processed. I received a letter from the IRS *five days* later saying that I'd been approved. "Bike Through Traffic" was officially a 501(c)(3) nonprofit organization!

I was in such shock that I called the IRS and asked if this was real. They assured me it was. When I told them I'd received an answer in five days, they said, "We did what?!" The fastest they'd ever approved a request was one month. God made ours happen in five days. In addition to that miracle, I'd also saved a couple thousand dollars in expenses because I'd done most of the work myself. I'd only had to pay the IRS submission fee.

From that point—when God showed His power over the IRS—I knew this was the path Christ wanted me to follow.

*My Family (Vince (Brother), Linda Joy (Mom), Jesaja (Brother), Daniel (me))*
*(Photo cred: Crystal Rose Photography)*

# Kissing Lions

*"When God tells you to run full speed into a brick wall, then trust that He will make a hole."*

~ Andy Stanley

Day 1 – Colorado

**April 19, 2015**

I left my home in Colorado and pedaled east toward Maine. I dipped down through Kansas and Oklahoma, stair-stepped up to Chicago, made it to Bangor, Maine, and zigzagged my way down the east coast to Miami. I biked up to Atlanta then ventured west, hitting all the major cities in Texas and into San Diego, California. From there I went north along the coast to Seattle, stair-stepped again through Montana into Utah, and then I kept pedaling east, back home to Colorado, where I arrived exhausted but thrilled on July 2, 2016.

During this tour, I met people whom I secretly referred to as lions. They were the kinds of people most of us wouldn't normally approach because they're perceived to be as fearsome as lions. To me, these "scary" people were drug dealers, pimps, murderers, and gang members. Yet that's who I kept meeting over and over on my tour. God impressed upon me a phrase that guided me throughout my trip: "kissing lions."

Now, I didn't take that literally. Rather, I realized that kissing is a sign of love and affection and that to kiss someone means you have to get close to someone to do so. You can't kiss from a distance. "Kissing lions" meant I needed to love these people just like Jesus did, and I didn't have to fear them. Even though they may have looked different and acted differently than me, we were still the same: just people in need of a savior.

What follows throughout this book are the selected stories of my many encounters during those 440 days covering 12,608 miles on a bicycle to raise awareness about domestic sex trafficking.

These are the stories of how I kissed the lions.

## The First Day of the Tour

I know that I am about to leave my home for fifteen months to ride a bicycle around the United States to raise awareness about sex trafficking. I know that my bicycle will attract more attention and give me a wider platform of people to reach, rather than a car. Sophia is my attention grabber. I know that I need to reach men and get them involved in fighting sex trafficking. I have the training, but my body trembles. I might even puke because I have no idea how this journey is going to turn out.

An intense spiritual battle seems to be going on. I don't know what to do or what I've gotten myself into. I argue with myself:

*What in the world are you even thinking to do such an outlandish excursion? How can I get out of this predicament I've created? Nothing's going the way I want it to. Everything I thought would be the easiest—like finding a place to sleep—has turned out to be the hardest. What am I going to eat? How will I support myself for the next year? Dear God, why did you let me agree to this?*

Prior to my launch, I'd sent out 340 personal letters to churches between Colorado and Oklahoma, asking if they could either host me or let me speak at a worship service or event.

Three replied.

Two flat out said no. The third said to call them once I got to Oklahoma. That's a success rate of 0.009 percent, and I rounded up.

Fundraising had taken a dive as well. I projected that I'd need roughly ten thousand dollars to cover my expenses for fifteen months. That included food, gear, and emergency funds. I left with all my gear paid for either through sponsors or stuff that I already owned, which was a blessing. I left Colorado with only $531 in the bank, 102 pounds of gear (including the bike) and two legs that'd had only three months of real training.

Why did I think this was such a good idea six months ago?

At my going-away party, which we held immediately before my launch, I make a repetitive speech because I couldn't find the right words to say. All that goes through my mind is, *Oh crap,* as if it were a record stuck in a loop. Before I leave, we gather in the front yard, and a dear friend of mine prays a powerful prayer over me while the rest of the group lays their hands upon me.

Twenty or so people line up with me, ready to ride alongside me for the first mile down to the local swimming hole. Nearly a hundred people begin counting: ten, nine, eight... My heart races and my body convulses. Five, four, my brain's not functioning. I'm unable to comprehend what's happening. Two, one.

In what's best described as a robotic wobble, I hop onto my fully loaded, 102-pound steel steed which I had named Sophia that I'm determined to ride for the freedom of those enslaved.

At the fairgrounds park, I realize I've forgotten my cell phone, wallet, Chaco's, and a couple of other important things. Great start, Lemke. Luckily, we only headed down to Longmont for the night (about twenty miles). My best friends, Caleb and Aishlinn, bring me the bag-o-stuff I'd forgotten.

When I arrive at my host's home in Longmont, Colorado that night, my heart settles and I'm able to focus.

Looking back now, this was just the beginning of what would become a drawn-out spiritual, mental, and physical battle that I'd have to endure for the entirety of my tour.

I was still in a place that was close to home and hanging out with some of my best friends. The reality of what this tour would entail hadn't fully set in. I mean I had really only gone twenty miles. As we sat together around a campfire eating hot dogs, I was trying to collect my thoughts while still enjoying my last few moments with my best friends and long-time spiritual mentor. In a comfortable state of mind, I closed my eyes for the night.

## April 20, 2015: Day 2 - Denver

We wake up and meet for breakfast with a lady named Jo who works for Love146, a nonprofit fighting sex trafficking. Our conversation consists of how we could partner together and what sex trafficking looks like from a local standpoint. We discuss what Love146 is doing to combat the problem.

## April 21, 2015: Day 3 – Colorado Springs

My host in Denver, Chelsea, treats us to Snooze, a local breakfast restaurant with amazing food. I head down to Colorado Springs and meet with a local newspaper reporter at the top of a 9.9 percent grade hill. It's the last quarter-mile of a sixty-four-mile bike ride, and as I look up the hill toward the reporter, I think, *My legs are burning, but I can't stop cause they'll think I'm pathetic.* Thankfully, I make it up the hill.

Later, God provides a place for me to shower and even get a free massage at the Colorado Institute of Massage Therapy. That night, I stay at Mrs. Blake's. She's a friend from camp, so I still don't realize that I'm actually on tour and leaving everything I've known far behind.

Essentially, I'm still training for what's to come.

## April 22, 2015: Day 4 - Nowhere

With intentions to ride to Rocky Ford, Colorado, I ride east. It's tough trying to find a close enough city and a long enough ride for the day. Eastern Colorado is, well, desolate. Upon arriving in Rocky Ford, I realize it's not the place I wanted to go. I continue riding east into an open abyss of nothingness.

Seventy miles later, I pull off on the side of the road to camp out. I'm exhausted and alone in the eastern plains of Colorado. I have no cellphone service, I'm running low on water, and I only have one Clif bar. The closest town is forty miles away. So, I set up my tent just ten feet from the highway. Any farther and I'll be part of a barbwire fence. I lay down to sleep, but my mind keeps me awake.

*This is idiotic. I should give up. It wouldn't be hard to do. Not from here. I'm still close enough to home that I could call someone and get a ride back. If I had cell service. Whatever. I'll bike in the morning and call someone. I can just pretend that my last year of planning never happened. People will understand. I can go back to working another dead-end job so I can repay all the sponsors and donors who've already given to me.*

The stench of cows infiltrates my tent. Coyotes howl and I swear they're just on the other side of the barbwire fence. Bats buffet my tent. Semis roar by. I think mice are trying to chew their way into my slightly warmer home. But I don't really notice any of it. These distractions cannot silence the question that's haunted me and begins yelling itself within my mind.

*Why am I here?*

I mentally beat myself up.

I struggle to fall asleep, and I'm not sure I ever really do. Despite being exhausted from the ride, semi trucks constantly race by my tent. My coyote friends howl relentlessly. I want to sleep, but the noises of the night and the noise of my mind keeps me awake.

Honestly, a small part of me wants one semi to veer off the road and hit my tent with me still in it.

## April 24, 2015: Day 6 - Lamar

Surprisingly, I wake up with a huge sense of joy ready to take on the day. I punctured my tube yesterday, but God kept it inflated for thirty miles until I arrived safely in Kit Carson, Colorado. I fix my tire and ride

34

on to Lamar.

A local church offers to put me in a hotel for the night but doesn't meet with me because they're busy. However, I get to meet a youth pastor from another church. We mainly talk about farming, but it's a great time to pour into someone else. This is the first stranger I get to talk to about my mission. After our talk, because I'm overwhelmed and the immensity of what I've set out to do is setting in, I'm extremely exhausted and discouraged. I can't pedal fast enough to flee my nagging doubt: *Why am I here?*

## April 25, 2015: Day 7 - Syracuse

I cross my first state line into Syracuse, Kansas, planning to meet up with a pastor who'd offered to put me up in a hotel that night. As I get into town, I find the pastor and we venture to the local hotel. To our surprise, it's closed.

Syracuse is a small town with a little over seventeen hundred people. It only has one hotel. Well, had one hotel.

As we scratch our heads trying to figure out what's going on, we decide to get some food and figure out our next plan of action. We don't have to walk far. The restaurants next door to the hotel.

Immediately after opening the doors to this dining establishment, we're greeted by a short, stern lady in her mid-sixties with shoulder length grey hair, a smile that could bring joy to any situation, a take charge attitude, and beautiful eyes filled with peace, love, and a past of wisdom and experience. She speaks before either of us do, "Do you need a place to stay?"

That's when my trip changed. That's when my purpose began to reveal itself, even if just slightly. That's when I have my first

35

unforgettable encounter on this crazy tour.

How does she know that? I'm at a loss for words, a rare event for me.

She continues, "I saw you looking at the hotel. The owner died two days ago. My name is Grandma Gay. You can stay at my house."

I try to process what she's saying. In my mind, it gets translated to: *Gay owner died in hotel. No, wait! Grandma is gay, killed hotel owner. No, that's not right. Hotel died, Grandma Gay offering room. Close enough!"*

Finally, I speak. "Did you say your name was Grandma—?"

"Yep, Gay."

I smile but try to hide it. "I'd love to stay with you, but . . . I need food first."

Later, I tell her that a buddy of mine named Micah is coming to meet me in Syracuse to ride with me for the next week. Grandma Gay's huge heart leaps at the opportunity to have more people over at her house. Once Micah joins us, we head to her house. From that point on, we feel as if we're her children.

She takes us around town and tells us her testimony. She had several grown children of her own, but one had recently committed suicide. She was now raising her grandkids, the children her son had left behind. Later, at her house, a five-year-old boy immediately attaches himself to Micah and me. He follows us everywhere. We're taken off guard and don't know what to do other than try to provide some fun and give him our attention.

Grandma Gay takes us to meet all of her kids. They look at us like we're going to rob her. They keep pulling her aside to ask if she's going insane for taking in two strangers.

She just responds, "It's what we as Christians are called to do."

## To Be Like Grandma Gay

Grandma Gay was no lion to be feared; she was a lioness of the faith to emulate. She reminded me of why I'd set out on this crazy tour in the first place: I wanted to meet people where they were at, to put the needs of others before my own, and to build people up. Grandma Gay was an incredible example of what it meant to meet people where they are and to lay down your life for the needs of others. In her eyes, Micah and I weren't strangers. We were souls in desperate need of care. Without a second thought, Grandma Gay offered us everything she had.

I continued from there with my head held high. I wish I could tell you that I never thought about quitting again after that, but, truthfully, I still had sometimes-daily thoughts of giving up. But now I know that if I'd quit so early, every seed God had planted in others' lives through me might still be waiting for water.

I also realized that the task before me was specifically bestowed upon me to live out. It was my responsibility to see it to the end, and I couldn't give up because I thought the task would require too much of me. By day eight, we'd left Grandma Gay's house after church and headed to Holcomb, Kansas. The pastor who had originally tried to get a hotel for Micah and I allowed me to speak at his church that morning.

In five minutes, I gave my testimony and God opened a door for me to talk about the hospitality of Grandma Gay, a woman whose name and spirit I will never forget.

# Journal Entry:
# Stripper Poles to Church Pews

Day 54 – Michigan

## June 11, 2015

I met a man a while back who used to own a strip club in Colorado. When we met at a seminar where I was a speaker, Brett's T-shirt captivated me. It read: "Jesus loves strippers." His smile and charm lured me in like a mouse to cheese. I asked Brett what he was doing at this seminar, and he simply said, "I turned a strip club into a church." Intrigued, I asked to know more.

In the early 80's, Brett started a strip club. In his mind, the club was a place to gather around, have some great laughs, eat decent food, drink your face off, and release some stress by looking at beautiful women. His club was a legitimate business with clean girls and big bouncers who would protect his girls from men trying to get too familiar with them. All the girls could pick their own hours, and most of the time they made well over $60,000 a year. Occasionally, he'd have an issue with his girls abusing drugs, but he thought it was normal and would try to get them help if they needed it. Business was booming, and once pornography hit the Internet in the early 90's, his business took off like a kite in a hurricane.

His son eventually got into the business and continued his legacy. They introduced new marketing ideas to publicize the strip club more and even did community service outreach with their girls to help promote the business.

A couple of years after running the business as a father-son duo, Brett's granddaughter came to him asking for a job. Brett laughed. "No way, you are my granddaughter. I don't want you stripping here."

At that moment, it was as if a train had just derailed or an earthquake was dividing his heart. Brett thought to himself, "Wait a second, these girls who are stripping in my facility are not just girls I've hired. They're also someone's granddaughter, daughter, sister, or mother." Brett couldn't sit by knowing that these girls in his strip club were someone else's loved ones. He didn't want his own family stripping at the club, so why would he allow anyone else's to strip there?

The next week he went to his local church and asked the head pastor if they could use the building for anything church-related. As God had planned it, that church had wanted to start a church close to the local University to reach college students better.

Brett sold the building to the church for pennies on the dollar. Now the church uses it as a college outreach center and a counseling facility for people with sex addictions and sexual trauma.

For Love,

Daniel Lemke

# Meeting the Problem in Person

*"While Jesus was having dinner at Matthew's house, many tax collectors and sinners came and ate with him and his disciples. When the Pharisees saw this, they asked his disciples, "Why does your teacher eat with tax collectors and sinners?" On hearing this, Jesus said, "It is not the healthy who need a doctor, but the sick. But go and learn what this means: 'I desire mercy, not sacrifice.' For I have not come to call the righteous, but sinners."*

~ The Bible (NIV) Matthew 9: 10-13


Day 152 – South Carolina


**September 18, 2015**

I stayed with a pimp.

The most common question I'm asked about this experience is, "How did you get to stay in a pimp's house?" The follow-up question is usually,

"How did you keep from punching him in the face?"

My short answer? Jesus.

If I'm being honest, I have no idea how I was able to stay in the homes of pimps, Hell's Angels, Skinheads, or porn producers, just to name a few. All I know is that I had a willing heart to show Christ to these people.

I used a website called "Couch Surfing (CS)" that allows travelers to find hosts anywhere in the world. Couch Surfing is free, and each host (as well as each surfer) has a profile and references from those who've used the service.

Through Couch Surfing, God opened the doors for me to stay with these people. Now, please don't think that Couch Surfing is filled with these kinds of people. It's an excellent website filled with amazing people. From my experience, the hosting "lions" on that site are maybe 1 percent of 1 percent.

## My New Pimp Friend

I stayed with Dillon, which isn't his real name, for two nights. Initially, I didn't know he was a pimp. As soon as I crossed the threshold of his home, I knew I needed to get to the heart of things with Dillon. The first words out of my mouth weren't, "Hi, how are you?" Rather, I purposefully chose for my first words to set me aside from all the other social lemmings Dillon had likely met so that he'd know I was different. I asked him a seemingly strange question, but it set the mood and realization that I wasn't there to have a boring conversation.

"How long is an elephant's trunk?"

Weird, I know, but you'd be surprised at how different of a

41

conversation follows after asking a question like that. I wanted to quickly get beyond surface-level with Dillon.

That simple question set me apart and allowed me to get to his heart faster than normal. I was sincere and intentional with my following questions. I didn't know why I was asking him these questions, or even why God wanted me to dive so deep so quickly, but as I stood there in his living room in my sweaty Star Wars T-shirt and bike shorts, I asked him questions like, "What was your childhood like?" "What brings you joy?" and, "What determines your life philosophy?" Still not knowing what he did for a living, I was determined to get this man to open up.

The best part was that he welcomed and answered every one of my questions in great detail. He had no resentment or hindrance toward my curiosity.

After a couple of hours, his profession finally revealed itself: "I'm an urges provider."

I quickly realized where the conversation needed to go. "What does that mean, exactly?"

"I'm in the exotic film business. I manage Tricksters. I provide for . . . urges."

Tricksters, in his world, were prostitutes on the streets who called their sex acts "tricks." I realized why Christ had put me in his house. I kept my same outlook toward him, determined to share the gospel with this man and love on him the way Christ would. When I first went into his house, peace settled upon my heart. This allowed me to keep the same attitude toward Dillon.

## "How Do You Find Them?"

We talked for a couple of hours and went for a tour around town. He took me to a fancy restaurant where we ordered steaks. My steak was terrible, there was more fat than meat, and it was super tough, but I sat there and soaked in every word he had to say.

I had two questions that had been bugging me: "How do you find your girls, and how do you get them to do what you want?"

In so many words, Dillon replied without hesitation: "I'll go to malls or public areas. If I see a girl sitting alone, I'll walk up to her and start complimenting her on her clothes. If she replies with a confident-enough response, I'll move on. I can't play into the emotions of a girl like that. But if I give another girl the same kind of compliments and she's unsure of herself, or she's shy and looking down, or if she starts degrading herself, then I know I can get her."

Then Dillon went into stories about some of the girls he had. He became enraged while talking about the parents of his girls. "They neglect their daughters. I'm a good man for taking them in when no one else will. I'm the only one in the world who provides for them and loves them."

In Dillon's eyes, he's a hero to these girls.

I was shocked and amazed, but I wanted to know more. "How do you get them to pull tricks for you?"

"Respect. They respect me. They turn tricks because I ask them to and they respect me."

I can only assume that Dillon's charm, his way with words, and his provision of their basic needs led to "his girls" obeying out of "respect".

43

Dillon acted like their boyfriend. To some, he even acted like their father figure. He was fully convinced that he was helping them, and he had the victims convinced they were in love with him.

"What about boys who play tricks?"

"I've never liked that. But I've got friends in the business that only prefer boys. I get asked all the time by clients if I have any boys. I don't."

"How much does each of your girls earn on a given night?"

I think Dillon's chest swelled with pride. "One hundred a session. My girls are quality."

Let's break that down: if one girl pulls one hundred dollars a trick and performs three-to-six tricks a day (that is low-balling it), she'll make three hundred to six hundred dollars a day. Now, let's say she'll work twenty-one days out of the month. On average, that's $6,300 to $12,600 a month!

Dillon's annual salary is anywhere from $75,600 to $151,200 for *one girl*, untaxed.

## Less than Dust

Just from hanging out with Dillon for the short time that I did, I could see why a young child, or anyone for that fact, would be enticed by his charm. It comes so naturally to him. He speaks with confidence and has such a way with his words. They suck you in like a fly to a bug zapper. This is why the beast of sex trafficking is extremely difficult to combat: manipulation experts are in charge.

To better understand this unseen world, it helps to know some of the terminology:

- **Pimp:** a man who controls prostitutes and arranges clients for them. They take part of their prostitutes' earnings in return.
    1. **Romeo:** A pimp who controls a person through psychological manipulation. Gives them gifts and affection.
    2. **Gorilla:** A pimp who controls a victim almost entirely through physical violence or force.
- **Madame:** A female pimp.
- **john**: the client, aka the purchaser of the sex slave.
- **Victim:** the sex slave, which could be a child or adult, male or female. Often we see them as prostitutes, porn stars, or strippers.
- **Chicken:** Underage boy.
- **Chicken Hawk:** Men looking for underage boys.
- **Twink:** Refers to victims roughly between the age of 15-24 years.
- **Bottom Bitch:** an American term for a prostitute who sits atop the hierarchy of prostitutes working for a particular pimp.
- **Sparrow:** a rescued victim, a survivor of sex trafficking.

An August 2005 article on the Federation for American Immigration Reform's website, "Human Trafficking—Exploitation of Illegal Aliens," reveals the breadth of the problem: "After drug dealing, human trafficking is tied with the illegal arms industry as the second largest criminal industry in the world today, and it is the fastest growing." When the article was written sex trafficking was projected to surpass drug trafficking in terms of breadth in ten years.[2]

Human trafficking has three subcategories: labor trafficking, sex trafficking, and organ trafficking.

My focus is domestic child sex trafficking, so let's start there.

# What is Domestic Child Sex Trafficking?

*"You may choose to look the other way but you can never say again*

*that you did not know."*

~William Wilberforce

The legal definition of human trafficking, per the Department of Homeland Security's website on human trafficking, is "a form of modern-day slavery, and involves the use of force, fraud, or coercion to exploit human beings for some type of labor or commercial sex purpose." Force, fraud, or coercion can also be respectively described as violence, trickery, or manipulation.[3]

In the book titled The Facts: What is Sex Trafficking and How Widespread Is It, Focus on the Family offers the best definition of these terrible crimes. "Child sex trafficking includes any child involved in commercial sex. Sex traffickers frequently target vulnerable people with histories of abuse and then use violence, threats, lies, false promises, debt bondage, or other forms of control and manipulation to keep their victims trapped.

"Sex trafficking happens within the larger commercial sex trade (prostitution, pornography), often at much larger rates than most people realize or understand. Sex trafficking has been found in venues scattered across the overall sex industry, including residential brothels, hostess clubs, online escort services, fake massage businesses, strip clubs, and street prostitution." [4]

From my experience on my tour, sex trafficking is everywhere, even in places you wouldn't suspect, like coffeehouses and sporting events.

Per the Polaris Project's online article titled Sex Trafficking, "Under U.S. federal law, any minor under the age of 18 years induced into commercial sex is a victim of sex trafficking—regardless of whether or not the trafficker used force, fraud, or coercion." [5]

Child sex trafficking includes any child under the age of eighteen who is involved in a commercial sex act (anything of value in exchange for sex, i.e., a place to sleep, food, jewelry, a toy). There wasn't a U.S. law until 2000, when the Trafficking Victims Protection Act (TVPA) became law. Roughly every two years the TVPA is reauthorized.

The average age of a child sold into sex trafficking is twelve to fourteen years old. This average includes teenagers and children as young as one year old. A child will be sold anywhere between five to ten times a night for anywhere between five dollars up to two hundred dollars if they've never been sold before. Many times, they're either given a new name or a number to identify them and are then put on a menu so johns can purchase them. In other words, they're inanimate objects sold like meat at a restaurant. [6]

There is no one specific race, or gender of a victim that is trafficked more or less than another. Same with those who are pimping.

"Since 2007, the National Human Trafficking Hotline, operated by

Polaris, has received reports of 22,191 sex trafficking cases inside the United States"— those are only the ones that got reported.[5]

## How Does Sex Trafficking Happen?

At what point in time does it become "trafficking"? How can someone determine the difference between forced sex versus consensual sex?

Trafficking occurs when the employer or pimp uses the act of stripping, nude dancing, or even hosting as a forced means of physical or sexual abuse. They will also restrict movement and communication with friends and family, which can mean that the sex-trafficked victim is under constant surveillance.

Sex trafficking can also happen through fraud, e.g., false promises of a different job, misrepresentation of working conditions, wages being taken away or lessened without notice, immigration benefits, altered or bogus contracts, non-payment, underpayment, or confiscation of wages.

Another sign of trafficking is coercion to compel an adult worker to engage in commercial sex with club patrons. This could be exploitation of foreign nationals, who may be unfamiliar with the language, laws, and customs of the country. Or it could happen through verbal and psychological abuse, threats of harm to the victim or the victim's family or friends, threats of deportation, lack of control over a schedule, isolation from the outside world, confiscation of passports and visas, debt increased through various fees to the club, pimp, or whatever type of system they've gotten into.[7]

Individuals who are working as a hostess, serving drinks, or dancing in these types of clubs may also be a type of labor trafficking if force, fraud, or coercion was used to induce the individuals into performing some form of labor or service.

It's a difficult line to determine, but if someone is aware of the signs of human trafficking, then it makes it much easier to spot and convict the person or persons responsible for conducting these crimes.

When a slave is first bought, an initiation known as the "Break-in Period" occurs. During this time, a child may be used as much as thirty to forty times in a single day and systematically gang-raped. The owners use this method to make the victim feel completely worthless and to indicate control. It proves to the slave that there is little that they can do and that their life is going to be even more of a living hell than it already is if they don't cooperate with their owner.

This is also when the slave will make their pimp the most money because the slave is considered "fresh meat," which makes johns want them even more, so they'll pay a higher price for the newcomer.

Not only is it horrific enough for these victims to be constantly abused by hundreds of different men and women each day, but these children are usually forced to take illegal drugs so that they're more likely to perform these hideous acts and less likely to fight back. A drug addiction is also a source of dependence on the trafficker because the slave can only get drugs from the trafficker, which gives the pimp even more leverage. Occasionally, a pimp can get a slave to work only for drugs rather than money. Most of the time, the trafficker doesn't even have to pay for the drug—the johns will supply them.[7]

## The Business of Sex Trafficking

One main reason drug dealers turn from selling drugs to selling people is because they don't have to pay for supplies. They coerce people into making them feel good, acting like a boyfriend or father figure, and eventually start selling the "product" (the child), which they didn't have to pay for in the first place and can reuse over and over again.

Traffickers will treat slaves as if they're nothing more than collateral. In the trafficker's eyes, they view people as supply and demand. Just like all businesses, they need to constantly make new products or bring in new ideas to keep their customers happy. Clients don't want to use the same child all the time, so they trade their victims with other traffickers. A child may be in Texas one week, Mexico the next, then Michigan, and so forth. The "owner" of the business doesn't care where the child is going or how they feel, because the child is a dollar sign in the pimp's eyes.

A business and marketing process goes along with this crisis, such as how people are placed into this system of corruption. There are hundreds of different ways someone may become trafficked, but let's start with the most common: the "opportunity abroad" scam.

After reading about an "opportunity abroad," a person will think they're getting the chance to make a better life for themselves and their family (if someone in their family isn't the one selling them for sex). The recruiter will convince the victim that they're going to get a great job, make a great deal of money, and even send some cash back home to their family.

The specific job they use to lure the victim can be just about anything, from acting to waiting tables. Someone whom they don't really know in another country offers them a great job but as soon as they arrive they're forced into sex trafficking and can't get out. They're threatened that they'll be killed. Or, if they were sent to the different country by their family, the trafficker will tell the victim's family that they were being disrespectful, which would make the family disappointed in the child because they threw away "an opportunity of a lifetime." In most cases, the slave only makes twelve to fifteen dollars a month—hardly enough to send any back to their family.[8]

Another issue that keeps slaves in the business is that most of them are brought into a country illegally. In other words, to the government of the country that they came to, they are illegal aliens, even if someone else forced them there. It doesn't matter to the country. In such instances, the slave is stuck in a lose-lose situation. If they run away, they won't be able to find a job because they're illegal, and the chances of them even speaking the same language as the country they've been taken to is slim. Victims aren't always taken by a complete stranger, in fact 46 percent of the time they're lured away by someone they already know.

Some victims may run away from home because of a poor living situation or out of rebellion. They are lured by someone who takes them in, treats them nicely, and takes care of them. Eventually, they become comfortable with that person and are brainwashed by the caretaker into sex trafficking. They're made to think such work is perfectly okay and a great way to make money. The person who once showed them kindness and brought the runaway under their wing becomes the runaway's pimp.[9]

## Bringing Justice to Sex Traffickers

Many times, especially in runaway scenarios, a victim will develop a love for their pimp and not see himself or herself as a victim. They're free to go, there's no abuse, and the pimp provides everything the victim needs. The trafficker has their victim convinced that having sex with strangers is what love is and that's how the pimp can provide such nice things for them. The victim sees the pimp as a good guy, or what we call a "Romeo Pimp." This is known as "Stockholm Syndrome," when a slave comes to believe they love their captor. You'll hear some of their stories within this book.

This makes the job of law enforcement difficult because, legally, if the victim is over eighteen years of age, the police can't do much since there are no signs of force, coercion, or fraud. From all external perspectives, the "relationship" is consensual. [10]

Convicting these criminals is extremely difficult. Many victims won't talk to the authorities because they live in constant fear for their lives or they believe they are in love with their captors. Some cases may even be swept under the rug because the authorities are paid off by a trafficker. And with culprits using the Internet to lure victims more often, it's even more difficult to track them down.

Remember the story of the Madame who fired me up to start combating sex trafficking? She was investigated for two-and-a-half-years and was placed in prison for only four months. People are jailed and given greater punishments for not paying their taxes. Who knows what she's up to now.

There's something very wrong with this picture.

The reason it takes so long to investigate and prosecute these pimps is that they're good at what they do. A cop could sit in the lobby of a massage parlor while a pimp is at the desk. A john could walk in, get his "massage," and come back out. He'll place the money on the counter and then walk out. The pimp never touches the money and it is seen as a tip, like a tip jar at a coffee bar. The cop can't do anything because he had no hard evidence that anything happened.

When the cop goes to the back, he receives an actual massage. If he goes in with a wire, the victim will ask him to strip down fully. This will either reveal the wire, or, since an officer can't legally strip naked, he has to leave his underwear on. Now the victim knows to give him a real massage.

This business is booming, with demand drastically increasing. We simply do not have the police force to combat this issue.

Even against these odds, I was one guy on a bike and knew I needed to help.

# Riding the Wake

*"I have taught myself to dance while riding Sophia! Jesus and I have dance-offs. I think He lets me win. I also took my first 'sink shower'. I used toilet paper, which didn't dry me off very well. I will have to perfect this 'sink shower'.*

~Daniel Lemke (Journal Entry)


Day 9 – Kansas


**April 27, 2015**

I never knew how hard the wind could blow without the occurrence of a tornado or a hurricane. I would soon find out.

According to the pastors we met there, Dodge City, Kansas holds the record for the windiest city in America. Luckily, I had my buddy, Micah Mitchell, riding alongside me, battling the wind—and the day—with me. It's not until this day that I realize how important having a friend with me is.

In cycling culture, "the wake" is what we call the wind that forms into a raindrop pattern around a solo cyclist. When another cyclist rides in front of you, you're "riding in the wake." In the same way that a sedan stays behind a semi to conserve gas, a cyclist rides in another's wake to conserve energy. To ride by yourself in heavy winds, over a long period, is extremely tiring and potentially damaging to your muscles. The last thing I wanted was to experience any kind of serious physical problem. But, of course, the wind blew against us as we pedaled toward Dodge City.

With headwinds reaching thirty-two miles per hour, I wouldn't have been able to make the trip—let alone meet these pastors on time—had it not been for Micah's help.

On our way to Dodge, KS we exchange the lead position every couple of miles so the other can ride the wake and recuperate. But even having Micah with me, I'm completely beat by the time we arrive in Dodge City.

After five hours and sixty-two miles of braving incredible winds and forty-one-degree temps, we stagger into a Chinese buffet restaurant to speak with two pastors about sex trafficking. I can hardly stand and my vision keeps going in and out. I'm sure I'm going to faint at any moment. Suddenly, my body temperature drops. I start to shake uncontrollably. I try to stop my shakes while still holding a somewhat intelligent conversation.

All the while, I keep thinking, *If I'm this bad and Micah's here to help me, what would have happened had he not ridden with me? How am I ever going to get through this trip on these long stretches by myself? How will I ever get anywhere on time and in a healthy enough state to even talk? What have I gotten myself into?*

But I don't have long to consider those deep fears. The pastors we're meeting with are sharing some devastating stories.

Pastor Chris Connor has been heavily involved in fighting sex trafficking for the last fourteen years. He shares details of a local case involving a twenty-five-year-old woman who'd filmed herself having sex with children, some under the age of five, and who shared those videos through her Google Drive account. Thankfully, Google discovered the images and reported the pictures to the National Center for Missing and Exploited Children. Today, the woman is now serving twenty-one years in federal prison on one count of producing child pornography.[11]

I'm starkly reminded about why I've begun this trip.

## The Twelve

This morning, we meet with twelve more local pastors. I share my heart and my belief that Christians ought to be talking more about sex trafficking in places where it's not normally discussed, like schools and churches. The pastors nod their heads in silent agreement.

I feel like they're the perfect audience for this message: twelve pastors who oversee a large network of churches. My theory is that if I can influence such people of authority, then they will inform their respective networks of believers.

At that moment, I realize that one of my goals prior to going on the tour—talking to crowds of no less than five hundred—is pointless. I need to seek more one-on-one conversations so I can have a more intimate impact rather than attempting to sway a few people among a massive crowd. From Dodge City on, I plan to meet with people of authority, or those within some form of network, to inform them about sex trafficking so they can reach out to their field of influence.

Content with the discussions we had, Micah and I ride out of Dodge City and head for Sun City, Kansas, just seventy-five miles away. We plan to camp on the side of the road that night and eat Twizzlers to our hearts' content.

But that doesn't happen. At all.

## It's a Pratt Day

Our legs are shot, our butts raw, and our skin bubbles from sun blisters. The soreness from the previous day's ride makes it a struggle to put one foot in front of the other. Still, we trek toward Sun City in the hopes that God will intervene so we won't have to camp out in the desolate plains of Kansas.

But no less than fifteen miles later, Micah realizes his sleeping bag has fallen off his bike. We backtrack a mile or two but can't find it. We can't go all the way back because that will add an extra thirty miles to our seventy-five-mile journey. Struck down but not destroyed, we resume our progress toward Sun City. We joke about cuddling up in my sleeping bag or fashioning a sleeping bag for Micah out of my four pairs of clothes.

We stop at a truck stop in a city that probably has a population of thirty, including its dogs. While Micah and I inhale greasy burgers and flimsy fries, a trucker walks up to our table having overheard our conversation. He says something to the effect of, "I hear you boys need to find some supplies. Try Pratt, it's about the same distance as Sun City, maybe five miles further, but they'll have what you need."

We thank him.

"Oh, and you should know that there's some construction going on. If you take the marked detour around the construction, that'll add ten miles to your trip. But, I reckon you all can get through that construction zone without any problems, seeing as how you're on bikes."

58

Micah and I exchange glances. Never ones to pass up an opportunity to save time and energy, we agree on cycling toward Pratt and cutting through the construction zone. But, in hindsight, I think both of us were just agreeing with what we thought the other one was thinking.

Instead, we should have listened to our guts.

I guess the next sign should have been our warning. As soon as we step outside, I see that my bike's rear tire has been slashed.

We laugh because that's our only response by this point. On days like these, the wind is never at our backs. Everything's uphill and into the wind, even when we aren't moving.

## The Detour We Definitely Shouldn't Have Taken

After fixing the tire, roughly eight miles down the road, we come to the fork where the construction detour begins. Left with the decision to take the detour, and add several miles to our trip, or risk going through the construction site, we yell, "Adventure!"

Famous last words.

We have a grand time riding down the lonely, traffic-less road. We ride on the opposite side of the road, hooting and hollering and pretending that we're jumping over oncoming traffic. It's fun to swerve all over the place, but it's also quiet and peaceful.

We see the construction zone on the horizon. From afar, it looks as if we'll have no problem traversing it.

Thirteen miles later, we finally reach it. As we straddle our bikes with our front tires hitting the metal barricade, our hearts sink into our knees.

We stand atop what used to be a bridge. Below, we see cranes and tractors that look to be the size of field mice. If the barrier hadn't been there and had we not been paying attention, we would have become squished field mice after flying off its ledge. (E.T. comes to mind.)

Why had we trusted that strange trucker?

We slam our palms to our shaking heads and both let out loud sighs. I speak first. "Micah, what do you want to do?"

"We could try and walk down there and say, 'Um excuse me. We need to get through. Don't mind us.' Or we could go back."

With a chuckle in my voice, I reply, "Pull out the Twizzlers. It's Twizz time."

With an apple in one hand and a Twizzler in the other, we sit on the asphalt with our legs spread out in front and the hot sun beating down on us. I check my GPS to see if we'd missed any roads that could have gotten us to our location. I notice that if we travel across the nonexistent bridge for another two to three miles, we'd meet up with the detour route.

As I gaze across a field at the horizon, I point and say, "Hey, Micah. How far does that road look to you?"

"Maybe a quarter mile to a half mile?"

"Want to see if we can walk it and maybe carry our bikes?"

We backtrack a short distance to take a dirt road that partially crosses the field. We ride about a hundred yards until the potholes and loose gravel "road" abruptly end.

## Fighting the Fences

"Micah? What now?"

"Lets go... left."

"Sounds great. It's greener over there anyways."

With our bicycles by our sides, we push our heavy steeds over muddy ground and through tall grass. We weave in between thorn bushes and tumbleweeds. To our surprise, our adventure finally seems to be going well—other than our cut-up legs, sweat draining from every pore in our bodies, and the grass and sticks that keep getting caught in our gears, making loud clicking noises.

Eventually, of course, we meet yet another obstacle. "Hey, Daniel!" "Yeah, what's up?"

"Um, how heavy is your bike?"

I don't like the sound of that question. "A hundred and two pounds. Why?"

"Do you think we can lift that? There may or may not be a barbwire fence in our way."

"This will be interesting."

We have another choice to make in front of that tall fence: Do we take all our gear off of the bikes and hand them over, or do we leave the gear on and powerlift the bikes up and over the fence?

We're men, so what do you think we chose?

Micah climbs over and somehow doesn't cut himself. From the opposite side of the fence, he grabs the front of my bike as I hold onto the rear. With an awkward approach, we lift Sophia up and over the mountainous spikes. I cut my chest on the fence, but what's a manly moment without a little blood?

Micah's bike is lighter, but we're both exhausted. As we hoist his steel behemoth over the fence, it slips out of my hands, rebounds off the fence, and smacks Micah on the head. We laugh uncontrollably as we gather our composure and approach the situation again. The process works the second time, and we don't waste too much more blood.

Once our rides are over the fence, I have to get over. I think about taking a running start and jumping. I think about climbing one of the posts and hopping over, but I don't want to break the fence. Eventually, I find an area where the ground's been dug down just enough, so I try to army crawl under it. Everything is going splendidly—until my butt becomes lodged in the fence. Micah has to assist me. This is not a manly moment. And, the grass is not always greener on the other side. Just saying.

We laugh for a while longer and throw around more puns, hoping that barbwire fences are going to be a thing of the past. But not too much farther along in the field, we're met with another barbwire fence.

"Oh, well then. There's that situation. Again," I said.

"But now we're pros at this." Micah stated.

"Let's do it."

Quoting my version of Shakespeare in a terrible Scottish accent, I shout, "Bringeth down thou wall! We shalt not be conquered by thee!" Then, slipping into a deep caveman voice, I follow it up with, "We are man. Man will not stop."

Once again, we get our bikes and ourselves over the fence. But, of course, once we're both over the bloodthirsty fence with all our gear intact, we see a gate just fifty feet from where we were. Together, we shout "NOOOO!" to a seemingly uncaring universe.

Still, the Day of the Disastrous Detour isn't over.

## Bushwhacked

We take another Twizzler break to plan our trek to the other road. We realize it's much farther away than we'd anticipated. We walk for what seems like days until we come to a "Kansas mountain." A mound of rocks nine feet tall with two steel rods strategically placed upon them stand as a fortress, blocking the most direct path to our intended destination. But, determined to get back to riding before the sun sets, Micah and I vow not to let these railroad tracks get us off track.

We try taking a running start at the hill.

We looked like that scene in the Harry Potter movie, where Ron and Harry try to get to the train station by running headlong through the magical brick wall? They crash, and all their stuff flies everywhere because Dobby the House Elf has just closed off the gate.

As soon as we hit the rock mound, our bikes buckle and we both face-plant into the rocky hillside.

At that moment, my bike feels like it has gained four hundred pounds. I'm a toddler pulling a car. I can't get my bike on top of the tracks. With the rocks slipping out from under us and the sun beating down, the struggle is real. After almost thirty minutes, we finally reach the top and plant our proverbial white flag—whether in triumph over ascension or surrender to the day, I'm still not sure.

Standing on top and swimming in our own sweat, we look across and see the road we need to get to just a hop and a skip away. Our eyes then drift down to the other side of the tracks.

You have got to be kidding me.

With another large sigh, we see a giant line of thistle bushes running the length of the tracks—a nonstop wall for as long as we could see.

Thinking of one of my favorite movies, Braveheart, I am inspired to say the only words that cross my mind. With a jolt of excitement and a loud, deep, gravelly voice, I yell, "FOR THE KIDS!"

No sooner do those words leave my mouth, Micah and I are charging down the rocky side, headlong into the bushes, our bikes in tow. We leap into the bushes, and then . . . we're stuck like flies in honey.

Uncontrollable laughter overtakes us, again. There really is no turning back now. We're not even sure we can turn forward. So, we embrace our present, thorny situation.

"Micah, you still there? I can't see you through these thorns." "Yeah, man. They aren't magical bushes that make me disappear." "Whoa! What if they were?"

"That would be amazing, but also really weird. I'd hope they'd take me to Narnia or something cool like that."

We wiggle our way through and only come out with a few skin abrasions. With our heads held high and the road within throwing distance, we skip on. At the road, we dance like fools as car after car passes, honking their horns in a sort of cheer for our arrival. But our excitement quickly fades when we realize we still have forty miles to go and the sun is about to give its last call before it turns in for the night.

## The Final Stretch

Part of me hoped for the obstacles to stop there. The other part was thinking, "Bring it on." But I also knew that nothing about that day was likely going to go right.

By the time we arrive in Pratt, Kansas, we're beat. A friend I'd called earlier was able to find us a church that would allow us to sleep on the couches in their youth room. Yet, even so close to our destination, we were met with one last obstacle.

Maybe five miles from the church, all four lanes of traffic had come to a standstill due to a car accident. We couldn't ride on the sidewalks because there were no sidewalks. We weaved through the stopped cars and watched the first responders do their duty. When we were finally able to pass, we'd waited forty-two minutes.

By that point, the sun had long ago set. Our legs were cramping and causing near-unbearable pain. Our body temps had dropped, causing our muscles to get stiff. The last three or four miles of our detour into Pratt were miserable. At 10 p.m., after eighty-one miles and a day we both wanted to put to rest and never experience again, we bunked in the youth room. To add insult to injury, we looked at our maps that night and realized our detour of two miles had taken us almost two hours to traverse.

## The Only Reason I'd Ever Relive This Day

The church we arrived at was a cute little building with the youth room set aside from the church. We were greeted by the Pastor, who offered us food they had left over from their homeless ministry. They didn't have showers, so we did a "sink shower." Basically, you find a paper towel, some soap (if available), and a sink, and then you wash your body. It didn't take long for an authentic shower to become a luxury on my trip.

We rubbed Biofreeze on our legs, which is like Icy Hot but for horses. I wrapped myself up in my sleeping bag. Micah, who'd lost his sleeping bag at the very beginning of this incredibly bad day, used a jacket and my microfiber towel as a blanket. The church wasn't a five-star hotel, but it was everything we could have asked for at that moment. The beautiful part about the entire day was that I had a companion with me, even if he were only going to be with me for a short time.

Looking back, the toughest part of the whole trip was being alone. Having Micah with me for a week during the early part of my ride helped me transition into the tough times to come. I could just tell myself the stories of the *Day of the Disastrous Detour*.

Our conversations throughout that day were beyond fruitful and encouraging. They not only motivated me to keep on going, but they made it easier for me to share my struggles with someone else rather than having to bear my burdens alone. If I were to change one thing about the entire tour, I would have asked someone else to join me rather than going it alone.

We aren't meant to be alone.

And I would soon learn that lesson the hard way.

(Micah and Daniel)

67

# Johns Need Help Too

*I never thought that I could feel claustrophobic outside. A strange feeling but having a plethora of trees towering over you like a sand castle collapsing on an ant is very overwhelming. Don't get me wrong, I love trees, however for some reason in Maine the trees seem to be stacked together like soldiers in battle formation. Riding along the windy inland roads of Maine was a fun game of peek-a-boo with the cars that would bolt around the corners in the cold rain.*

~Daniel Lemke (journal entry)

Day 92 – Maine

## July 20, 2015

I've been on top of fourteeners (14,000-foot mountains) where I'm the tallest thing (since trees don't grow that high). I've had some close calls with lightning way up there, but Maine set a new record for me.

I maybe saw a car every hour or so due to the seclusion of the road I was on. It was about fifty-one degrees with an inconsistent rain. My beard collected water for me. I could just stick my tongue out, twirl it around, and lap up the droplets that had accumulated. While riding through a tunnel of trees, I'd see flashes of lightning but never the actual bolt—until Zeus said hello.

Remember that moment in *The Terminator* when Arnold Schwarzenegger is transported to the past (well, the present of 1984) and a ball of electricity surrounds him? Well, that's what this moment was like, except no one showed up naked afterward. My ears rang for days due to the eruption of thunder at that moment.

I've had my hair stand up only once before due to lightning being so close. That time in Maine, not only the hair on my head stood up but also my shoelaces perked up. My phone may even have jumped up in battery percentage. In a roundabout way, it's pretty sweet to think that when we're doing what God wants us to do, not even lightning can touch us.

Day 92 was a radical day on my tour that changed a lot in the way I think. Maybe it was lightning induced, but whatever happened, I changed. On that day, I got to stay with a very outspoken and unashamed john.

But, before I tell you about him, we need to act like Arnold and head back in time, to three weeks before Day 92.

## Dear John

A friend of mine and board member named Kristin helped me find hosts by reaching out to churches or people on Couch Surfer. She'd send out a brief overview of who I am along with a personalized note that looked something like this:

Dear (Enter Name),

I loved reading your profile. You seem to be extremely adventurous and know how to experience life! (PERSONALIZED MESSAGE HERE).

As for me, I am traveling 12,000 miles around America for 15 months on a bicycle to raise awareness about domestic sex trafficking. I have already done (enter your distance traveled). Now I am looking for a place to stay for the night so I can continue this journey!

If you want more info about the ride, you can check us out at www.BikeThruTraffic.com or Facebook.com/BikeThroughTraffic.

Hope your day is going well, and I look forward to hearing more of your stories!

For Freedom,

Daniel Lemke

I'd send this message out to roughly four or five hosts per city on Couch Surfing and call fifteen or so churches to find a host. I hate to say it, but the churches almost never hosted. I maybe had a five percent success rate with the church. After a while, I stopped calling churches and solely went to Couch Surfing, fire stations, and letting the Holy Spirit find me a place to stay.

Now, I get it: the church constantly has people asking them for things and it can become discouraging for them. It used to make me really mad that the church wasn't taking me in, but after a while, I realized that God had better plans for me. The church didn't need me, but the lions did. The lions needed to be shown the real church, not just the building.

Weeks before Day 92, Kristin had reached out to several people in Maine but failed to get much of a response. About three weeks out from traveling there, I was getting nervous about not knowing where I was going to sleep. Looking back, three weeks was a great window of time. As the tour progressed that window got smaller and smaller.

I got a phone call from Kristin. "Daniel, I don't know what you want to do here." "What are you talking about?"

"Go and check the last CS message from a guy named

Leonard." With a hint of curiosity and worry, I asked, "Is everything okay?"

"You'll see. Call me back once you've read it and let me know what you want me to say back."

We hung up and I rushed to my Couch Surfing app as I wheeled through the streets of upstate New York.

Hello Daniel,

My home is open to you. I have a camper out back for you to use, nice and private, and of course shower and kitchen, etc. I'm often busy, but I have no other guests scheduled then.

You might think twice, though. I am a man who has engaged the services of prostitutes on many occasions, I still do from time to time, and I am entirely unapologetic about it. I think it's quite natural. I am also quite doubtful, even critical, of the effectiveness of campaigns to "raise awareness" of any issue, especially when the method involves recreational activities.

I mean no offense, and I mean that sincerely. But neither do I choose my words with the aim of avoiding offending the listener. I find that gets in the way of truth telling. Let me know.

Yours,

Leonard

My jaw dragged on the pavement.

To my surprise, a rush of excitement overcame me. I was stoked to get to meet this guy and pour out Christ into his life. I had no idea what to expect or what to even talk about once I got there since I'd had no prior experience with a john, but I was willing to let God use me in the way he wanted. I called Kristin back.

"KRISTIN! Let's do this! I'm terrified yet pumped at the same time."

"I think it will be a great opportunity. You need to be praying about this and even post it to our Prayer Warrior group and let them know."

"Yes, ma'am."

We hung up. The conversation I had with Jesus afterward reflected my passion and willingness to meet people where they're at. I told Him about my fear and worry, but He assured me that if I went into this with fear, I'd fail. Fear is not of Christ, and I needed to show this man the entirety of Christ through His love. Later, I'd come to realize that Leonard was an extremely confident man in what he believed to be morally right and wrong. If I had been controlled by fear, I would have shuddered in his confidence and not been as bold as I needed to be.

Those three weeks until Day 92 were daunting. The enemy kept getting in my head and telling me lies about how I wasn't going to change this guy's mind or that he was going to harm me. I even had people back home tell me I shouldn't place myself in dangerous situations, but those were the same people who said I should have only stayed with Christians. My mind was a war zone. I knew Jesus told me not to be fearful and I saw why. I almost told Leonard I wasn't going to come. I almost lied and said I'd found another host.

The day before I rode to Leonard's house, I endured a terrible rainstorm. Lightning struck like a force field around me. At that moment, I realized that I was under the protection of Jesus Christ. If one billion volts of electricity couldn't harm me, then a man whom God put in my path couldn't even come close. Joy rushed through my veins and filled me up with excitement and anticipation to meet Leonard.

## "Sometimes, You Just Get Urges."

Riding to Leonard's house, I was anxious to get there until I hit the dirt road leading to his house in the middle of nowhere. I hate how cliché this situation seems, but understand: johns aren't always like this. Most of the time, they're the ones you least expect. Leonard's house was several miles outside of town down a long dirt road with trees crouching down on you as they guided you back to a standalone cabin at the end of the gravel. The house was an old, cockeyed, beaten-up, dark brown log cabin with random trinkets all around the property.

Leonard came out front to greet me and welcomed me into his home. He was a tall, slender, older gentleman with long white hair pulled back into a ponytail, yet slightly balding on top, with a patchy goatee and thick, black-rimmed glasses. Sort of a skinny, hipster Colonel Sanders. Excitement flooded me again, and with an enthusiastic handshake I greeted him while going into detail about my eventful ride that day.

We walked inside as if I'd been there before. Leonard had toured all over the world on bicycles, so he'd prepared an assortment of gourmet, home-cooked food that would be filling and nutritious for my body. He showed me around his house and said that while he prepared the main course, I should go and shower up.

I didn't want to shower. I wanted to start getting to the heart of things, but I also needed to clear my head and have some time to pray.

As I stood in the janky shower washing off crystallized electrolytes and splattered bugs from my body, I pleaded to Christ, "Father God, thank you for this opportunity. I have no idea why you have me here. What the heck am I even doing? You are in control, and I want you to be the one that takes over this conversation. Guide my words and let them be your words, not mine. Your will be done, Father. Use me the way you want to."

As the water rushed over my body, cleansing me, the Holy Spirit rushed over my mind, guiding it to enter into the conversation the way He wanted it to go. I got out of the shower feeling refreshed and ready to love Leonard to the best of my ability.

Almost immediately, we jumped into a conversation about his thoughts on prostitution. I may have been a little blunt with my questions. They left no room for waltzing around the topic.

"Hey, Leonard, you said in your email that you'd engaged with prostitutes on many occasions and that you think it's natural."

Leonard looked at me as if to say, *All right. We're doing this*. He went into detail about the bicycle tours he'd been on and the travels he'd done.

Then he said, "You know, Daniel, sometimes you just get urges that you need to have fulfilled."

I didn't say anything to that and chose to hear the rest of his story, which was fascinating. Leonard had once had a family, a wife, and two kids. They'd built a quadrem (four-seat) bike they'd use to tour across America. He was knowledgeable about holistic medicine, healthy food, and how to live on very little money. He'd also toured on a bicycle on just about every continent and was planning another tour to travel through Africa.

Later in life, his family left him. He didn't go into detail as to why.

Leonard fully believed in science, nihilism, and that God cannot exist. In his mind, all values or moral rights and wrongs are baseless. Nothing can be known or communicated, since we're such a tiny blip in the expansion of time, nothing we do matters. He believed that a God who has always been could never help him if he's only here for a short second.

I was thrilled to ask questions like, "Why do we see the effects of history if nothing that anyone does affects further generations?"

Later, as our conversation progressed from prostitution to religion to moral justice, Leonard's beliefs about prostitutes came up.

75

"My question for you, Leonard, is how did you find the prostitutes that you slept with?" "They usually found me. I mean, I know where to go most of the time."

Leonard then went on to talk about how he believes that everyone in prostitution chooses to be there—that it's of his or her own free will that they're in that situation.

This is one of the biggest lies in the sex industry. No one wakes up and says, "I want to be a prostitute." They are there due to forced circumstances that forever altered their lives.

Leonard told me of a friend of his who couldn't pay rent. She chose to sleep with the landlord to cover her rent.

In moments like that, I throw my hands up in the air and say, "Those people are not the ones I'm talking about, that scenario only refers to such a small fraction of those who are in the sex industry. A majority of the sex industry—prostitution, porn, etc.—are children, and in my opinion that is not okay."

Our conversation went on for about nine hours. We dove deep into so many different aspects of sex trafficking. I told him many stories about victims I'd worked with or had been told about.

I talked about the porn industry. Jesus came up all the time, and we'd often jump back and forth between sex trafficking and Jesus.

By the end of the night, we were both still extremely friendly with each other, periodically joking and laughing. We closed the evening with Leonard playing his mandolin. After the song was over, Leonard paused for a minute; a single candle in the room was the only thing illuminating our faces.

He said, "Daniel. Thank you. I really had no idea how much of a problem sex trafficking was. I know I told you that raising awareness is useless, but I think what you are doing is admirable."

My heart skipped ten beats. For me, that was the best compliment I could have ever heard. We said good night and I walked through his yard to the lone truck camper in the back. I could hardly sleep because I was so pumped from the conversation. I sang a loud song of praise to God as I punched the air in excitement from our talk. I couldn't believe Leonard had said what he did by the end of our talk. I laid my head on the pillow with a smile that went from ear to ear.

## Johns Need Help Too

Because I'd stayed with Leonard, he left a reference for me on Couch Surfer:

> *Daniel is a worthy young man; as a guest he has all the proper attributes. He stayed only overnight, yet we now know each other quite well due to his honest questions and honest answers. He is one of those rare people who leave you enhanced by the meeting. I'm a slightly better person now because of his example. I recommend that you host him if at all possible. Whoever you are, you need more people like Daniel in your life.*

More often than not, we don't think johns need help. Many people believe they should all die or be put in jail. I'm not saying they don't deserve to reap the consequences of their actions. What I want to get across is that they need help.

The psychological issues that pollute their minds are a disease and they need counseling to learn that what they're doing not only damages others but themselves as well. A huge disconnect exists in their minds. They think only of themselves: "I want to be pleasured. I have a need.

77

Me, me, me." They think they're helping prostitutes because they choose to believe the victim wants to be there. We need people to understand that 9.9 times out of ten, a prostitute doesn't choose to be a sex object. Johns need help to rehabilitate their thinking.

Thank you, Leonard, for giving me the opportunity to hear your story and letting me share the gospel with you.

# Long, Lonely Road

*"Jesus Christ did not say, 'Go into all the world and tell the world that it is quite right"* — C.S Lewis

Day – All day everyday

Studies show that the average attention span is—wait, I need to click on "Embarrassing Statistics."

Where was I?

Right. Studies show that the average attention span is eight to twelve seconds. Mine is probably three.

When I rode my bike for an average of five to eight hours a day, I had to keep my attention somewhere. Otherwise, I would have died! That might be a little exaggerated, but I did have to come up with interesting ways to keep my mind focused. Just sitting on a tiny bicycle seat for that long gets extremely monotonous.

A typical day for me went something like this:

## 7:30 a.m.

If and when I could, I'd try to wake up around 7:30 a.m., thinking that I'd leave by 8:30—which almost never happened. I'd try to have a large breakfast with my host and eat some form of starch and protein. Honey-drizzled oatmeal provided me with the longest-lasting amount of energy. Through that simple meal, I'd have enough fuel for almost my entire day's ride. If I ate that in the morning, I wouldn't stop for lunch and have to spend more money. By the time I'd arrive at my next host home, I would have barely expended all the calories from breakfast and the previous night's dinner.

After breakfast and final thoughts with the host from our conversations, I'd pack up my things and leave.

## 9:00 a.m.

Packing always took me a ridiculously long time. Even though I felt like I didn't have to pack much personally—I just needed to pack my bike shorts and shirt from the day before—all my gear had to be packed. All of my items had their specific places on my bike, too. If a couple of things were out of place, not everything would fit.

Every time I woke up and went to my bike to start packing, it was as if someone had thrown my gear all over the room. Many times I'd just wear the same clothes for the third or fourth day in a row because I didn't want to deal with the mess. I hardly had any clothes in the first place, so my clothes were always dirty with sweat and covered in kamikaze bug stains. But I also just didn't want to pack. Packing can be exhausting, especially if you have to do it every single day and especially if you're exhausted while doing it.

I tried so many different systems to help keep my stuff organized, but none of them ever seemed to work.

80

## 10:00 a.m.

By the time I finished packing and collecting my thoughts, it was usually close to 10 or 11 a.m. I'd hop on my steel beast and trudge the unknown road that lay before my rubber, Kevlar-lined tires. The hours seemed to always drag on without any end in sight, especially if the wind was pounding down like Thor's hammer, which was practically every single day.

The wind never seemed to blow in the direction I wanted it to. Even if I turned to ride in the opposite direction, three minutes later the wind would shift patterns and become a headwind, again. On average, I'd keep a pace of about fifteen miles per hour, and I'd travel about fifty to eighty miles per ride.

Within the first six minutes of almost every ride, I'd zone out or start playing a mental game to keep my focus. These "games" deserve their own section.

## Road Games

Sometimes I'd play "I spy" by myself, but I'd quickly forget what I'd originally picked out in the first place. That's a hard game to play solo.

I'd try to harmonize with the sound of my bike chain and belt crazy show tunes. I may have sung "I Wanna Be Like You" from *The Jungle Book* at full volume for miles upon miles, but only me and the open road know that for sure, and those people who gave me strange looks.

My prayer life became more of a conversation with my best friend. I'd do this sort of spoken-word prayer thing when I'd talk to Jesus. (I like to call spoken word the heavy metal of poetry.) I'd often be riding with Jesus and point out cool scenery or have Him tell me stories about the people I'd pass. I quickly learned how to have a conversation with

Him just like I would with any of my other friends. Sometimes we'd race or He would have me pull over to take in the surroundings because I'd often get tunnel vision and not look around as much as I would have liked.

As I'd cruise through a city, I'd set my vocal cords to eleven and yell some of the most random things I could think of. I can only imagine any spectators thinking, *What the heck just happened,* while seeing some guy riding through town and yelling things to no one. For me, it was a time to laugh at myself and keep my mind entertained.

Occasionally I'd try to dance while riding my bike. This may seem to be an impossible task, and, well, you're partly right, especially since my feet were locked into the pedals. However, I still attempted this feat many times. In my mind, I was a dancing king, but to the cars driving by I probably looked like a fool sporadically head-banging while flailing his arms around like a madman imitating a helicopter. If I had a good song in my headphones, I couldn't control my body. I let the music take control.

I'd keep from going insane through social experiments, too. If I arrived in a town that I was just passing through, I'd talk to the locals, but I'd use a silly pirate or Russian accent and ask, "Vare are ze peaches?" Most of the time they'd give me a blank look, but some kind souls would try to help me find a store with peaches. When I'd say that I wanted to eat a peach and they thought I said beach, things got very interesting.

I'd also walk into hardcore biker bars with my bicycle outfit on and order a whiskey. The looks I got were priceless, especially when I'd park my bicycle next to all the Harleys and try to blend in. When I left, I'd make motorcycle sounds as I pedaled down the road. If I were feeling spunky, I'd even "kick start" my bike and ride with my hands in the air like I was riding ape hangers. I'd shout back, "Vroom, vroom!"

As far as the weather was concerned, I had to find ways to entertain myself while battling the elements. When it would rain, I'd open my mouth and try to catch raindrops. If I got one in my mouth, I'd gain a point. If one went in my eye, I'd lose a point. I usually ended up well into the negatives playing that game.

With the wind—after I stopped getting mad at it—I'd often pretend that I was in a war zone taking on giants. Or, I'd trick myself into thinking that I was actually going so fast that time was standing still and I was a racecar. In reality, I was standing still, because the wind was so brutal.

When hailstorms came, I could seldom if ever find shelter, so I'd pretend I was playing paintball with my friends. Even though marble-sized hail was pelting me, I had to find the joy in it. Otherwise, I'd be a grouchy man, which would hinder me from witnessing to others. One of the games I'd play after hailstorms was "Connect The Dots"— drawing lines to and from each of the welts on my body.

In the blistering heat, I'd often pretend I was lost on an island with very little water, or that I was trying to get through a desert. In reality, I ran out of water multiple times and had more heat strokes then I can remember, but I had to keep on going. The only way I knew how to find joy and endure was to make games throughout my day.

## Angel Dogs?

If there was one thing that always caught me off guard while I was riding, it was being chased by a dog.

One of my favorite dog-chase stories happened while I was riding in northern Florida. The hills were lush green and the trees were slightly swaying in the wind. Out of nowhere, a large, black, brown, and gray dog bolted down the hill perpendicular to me. In the quick second I needed to realize what was happening, my body tensed up and my heart ended up in my throat.

At the next moment, I saw the dog picking up speed. In fact, he sped up so much that once he reached the bottom of the hill, he ran straight into the ground and flipped over himself, barrel-rolling three or four times. I saw the dog's pride deflate as I passed. He hung his head in shame as if to say, "I meant to do that. I'll let you pass just this once, but next time . . . you'll be sorry."

I was laughing so hard that I had to pull over and collect myself. Joyous tears were blocking my vision.

Not all dogs are devils. Some of my dog stories make me wonder if God has angel dogs. During part of my ride through Missouri, the host I'd met through social media came to ride the second half of the day with me. During our ride, a black lab of some sort came out of nowhere and began running alongside us. Neither of us were scared or surprised when we saw her, she seemed to be a happy-go-lucky dog.

The black lab ran with us for a couple of miles until, about a hundred yards ahead of us, a larger black lab with snarling teeth charged us. Our dog saw the other dog charging and ran ahead. She crossed our path and ran right in front of the bigger dog. She stopped the aggressive dog right in his path.

She stared him down as if to say, "You will not harm my friends." The mean dog, its teeth still bared, cowered away as our companion stood with determination to defend my host and me as we rode by. She joined us again as we passed by. Maybe a half-mile down the road, she got distracted by armadillo roadkill. I can understand that.

It was amazing to see God protect us by using a dog.

## 5:00 p.m.

By the time I'd arrive at my host house in the evening, which could be as early as 3 p.m. and as late as 8 p.m., it was difficult for me to hold a casual conversations. My mind couldn't handle it. I had to make the conversation interesting and I think that is why my ministry was as effective as it was. If I didn't keep myself entertained, I would have given up much sooner. Riding for that many hours is, by far, the most boring thing anyone could ever do.

Often, when I arrived at my destination, I'd have some sort of speaking engagement, either with a small group, church, or a person of authority, i.e., someone in charge like a pastor, senator, police chief, CEO, etc. More often than not, I wouldn't get to eat until *after* the engagement, but that allowed me to really enjoy the company of my host. You can really get to know someone by the way they prepare food and eat.

Usually, if we had time after dinner, we'd explore the town. I'd talk the whole time about sex trafficking and try to get to my host's heart. After any shenanigans in town, we'd come back to the house. I'd try to catch up on emails and social media until around one in the morning. By the time I'd close my eyes for the night, I'd immediately pass out from exhaustion.

However, I still had many sleepless nights. I'd often wake up in the middle of the night with no idea of where I was. I'd freak out, thinking I was either back home or in a different state than I actually was. If I woke up thinking I was back home, I'd get scared because my surroundings were different and I had no idea how I'd gotten there. I'd wake up panting and in such a state of confusion that I'd sometimes yell

85

out in fear. Waking up and not knowing where I was seemed to happen at least one or two times a week, and each time, it would take me a minimum of six minutes to realize where I actually was.

As you can imagine, trying to adjust back to a normal life after playing all those games has been pretty difficult.

It's easy to see that my mind is imaginative. But you may be asking, "Why did you put yourself through all of this?" My answer is simple: I knew that if people were being bought and sold for the purpose of being abused by others, I couldn't just sit by. I knew that my short burst of terrible times couldn't match their lifetimes of misery.

I wanted to see the captives set free.

This is why I got back on my bicycle every day.

Jesus called me to do something, and I needed to do it—for the kids!

*Sophia blending in with the motorcycles*

*Daniel speaking at a men's conference in Texas*

# Impulse Buy

*"I have never seen New York. This is nothing like I was told it would be. But I am glad that I have all this experience of riding now because when a semi drives by inches from my shoulder at 60 miles per hour, I don't even notice it any more. New York will be a cakewalk. I could really go for some cake right now!"*

~ Daniel Lemke (journal entry)

Day 107 – New York

**August 8, 2015**

My destination hovers on the horizon, the city many refer to as the greatest city in America. It's one of the only cities in the US that gets its name confused with the entire state. It has a monument that was a gift from the French. It's a place where you can be anything you want to be—just as long as you have a bank account like Bill Gates. It's King Kong's playground and a cement truck's pride and joy. It's one of the few places on Earth where it'll take you two hours to go four miles in a car. This is a city where the only nature available is a small park in the middle of a brick jungle.

I'm in New York City.

As I come into the city overwhelmed by all the towers built to dance in the clouds, I have a craving for something I haven't thought about in years. The urge hasn't been this strong in a long time. I haven't even wanted to smoke in three years, but I have to get my grubby hands on a three-inch box of neatly wrapped cancer. Two blocks away from my host's home (an old friend from high school who was now a starving artist actress), I park my bike and bolt into a convenience store that reeks of body odor and marijuana.

"Got any Turkish Royals?"

"We have no."

I point to a red box behind the cashier. "Guess I'll take those, then."

"Fifteen thirty."

"For Marlboro Reds? I've never paid that much for them before." "Welcome to New York City."

I think, *So he's a comedian, too, and since when did cancer get so expensive?*

As soon as I leave the store, my desire to smoke vanishes like, well, smoke. Apparently, I just needed to buy expensive cancer sticks as a memento of my first trip to the Big Apple.

Since my host wasn't going to be home for a couple of hours, I wait for her at the end of a littered street that smells like urine. I claim a lamppost with a large cement base as my perch to investigate the locals.

Construction workers stand in the street. An ambulance races by every five minutes. Homeless people loot trashcans. Black kids swagger by, Arabs push a shopping cart toward a street vendor barking his

89

wares. A barber cuts a client's hair outside. An endless stream of people of all nationalities threaten to drown out every horn-honking car stuck in traffic.

Am I the only white kid in this area?

I'd been wondering why I was getting so many weird looks. I had automatically assumed it was a result of my tight black bike shorts, yellow bicycle jersey, and the loaded-down bicycle beside me. I stuck out like a yellow elephant in a fourth-grade classroom.

However, I'm not going to let that stop me from being me. I claim my post and continue to people-watch. Twenty minutes later, with my legs dangling off the edge and a jazz tune dancing in my head, a woman in her mid-thirties approaches me.

## Looking for Trouble

"Whatya doin', honey?" She scans me from head to toe.

Her purple high heels, smeared lipstick, and oversized T-shirt covered in coffee and dirt stains cause me to make certain assumptions.

She doesn't wait for my reply. "Got any plans tonight?"

"This is my first time in New York, so I thought I'd just people-watch for a while. How about you? Any plans?"

With mischief peeking out from behind her bloodshot eyes, she gives me a well-rehearsed statement as a question: "I'm looking for trouble?"

I smile. "If you're looking for trouble, there are some police officers over there. I'm sure they can help you find what you're looking for."

She laughs and looks at the ground. "No, silly. Not that kind of trouble." She raises one eye toward me. "You know what a girl needs."

"Does your need begin with the letter J and end with esus?"

Quickly becoming impatient and realizing her pathway toward finding a john is going nowhere with me, she leaves.

*Well, God, I tried.*

Well, Daniel, try again.

*Well, God, I don't have anything else to gi—*

I reach to my side remembering the pack of cigarettes I'd just bought. *So that's why my urge to get these was so strong. They're not for me.*

"Wait! Wait! Do you want a cigarette?"

She turns around, sees the tobacco sticks in my hand and a genuine smile spreads across her face. Without a word, I give her one, light it, and then light one for myself—for the cause.

Now that her immediate physical need has been met, I figure I can offer her something more. I tell her all about the one real need she'd ever need to have fulfilled and how that need is only met through the person of Jesus Christ. Eventually, I ask, "Do you know what love is?"

Now both of her eyes meet me as her brow furrows.

"My boyfriend loves me." Believing she had adequately answered my question (or giving up on chasing a new and unresponsive john) the conversation changes.

It's not sharing water at a well with a woman divorced five times over, but it's pretty close.

## Tabitha

"Tell me about your life, Tabitha." That wasn't her actual name, but it's a fitting alias. In Hebrew, Tabitha means "beauty" or "grace," and I think this Tabitha needed to know the true meanings of those words. I'd often ask such open-ended questions just to get people talking. I knew that getting to her heart would be where Christ could begin to do his work. I wondered if anyone had ever asked her these kinds of questions.

For reasons beyond me, I think God gave me the gift of comfort. I don't mean that I was comfortable on the road or in many of the circumstances I found myself in; rather, other people often feel comfortable talking to me about their lives. They would be honest and emotional and wouldn't hold back. Tabitha was no different.

Tabitha had grown up in a house of poverty with an alcoholic mother and an autistic sister. Her mother had no idea who her father was because so many men had been in and out of her life. Because of her mother's alcohol and drug addictions to pills and later to heroin, Tabitha's mother would sleep with men for money to fund her out-of-control desires.

This isn't even the worst part of her story, and a warning is in order: this is the brutal truth about how many prostitutes become hardwired to become sex slaves.

When Tabitha's mother didn't receive enough income, she'd tell her "boyfriends" to sleep with her daughters. She'd hint at it by telling her johns, "Go and comfort my daughters. Keep'em out of trouble." Then these men would pay for the opportunity to rape fifteen-year-old Tabitha and her autistic, eleven-year-old sister.

92

Tabitha thought she was helping her mother earn income because, to her, that's the way the world worked and the only way to pay the bills. When Tabitha would go to her mother with dreams of becoming a nurse or an architect, her mother would always tell her, "If that doesn't work out, at least you'll be able to sell your pussy."

## All Caught Up

Tabitha pauses after telling me all of this. Maybe she's surprised at how much she's revealing to a stranger. She looks at my cigarettes again and I gladly give her another one. She quietly asks, "Can I borrow your cell phone? I need to check in with my boyfriend."

I know what she means by boyfriend, but I don't want to take the chance of her running off with my phone if I hand it over, so I ask, "What's his number? I'll dial and put you on speaker."

Part of me wants to hear their conversation.

As soon as I hear the man on the other line speak, Tabitha's demeanor radically changes. She starts talking in a babyish tone intertwined with a hint of moaning. "Baby! When can I come home? I miss you."

The man plays into her emotions but with a distant yet sympathetic tone. "You know when you can come home. Are you all caught up?"

This guy is good.

I sit there trying to figure out how to convict this dude and yet he's so good at his job that he knows not to incriminate himself. Tabitha eats it up like a kid at a candy store.

*She's found someone who shows her enough care and provides for her, yet she's completely blind to how he's*

93

*using her.*

I want to yell into the phone, "I'm coming for you punk and when I find you I'm going to kill you." But I refrain.

Pimps can be trapped in a delusion of moral justification, but we as Christians still need to show them Christ through love, even when what they're doing perpetuates so much suffering. When I stayed with pimps or met them on the streets, their stories were often the same: "It's all I know." Their uncles, fathers, or mothers were pimps and essentially taught them the family business. Most if not all of them are trapped in that mindset and see their profession as morally justified. They see themselves as helping boys and girls out of terrible situations. For instance, Tabitha's "boyfriend" fully believes that he's providing a better situation for her, opposed to the life she was living before.

When her pimp hangs up and Tabitha drops her subservient act, I can tell she's enraged. I'm not sure by what, specifically, but I imagine it's because she thought she was done for the day, but now she won't be allowed "home" until she's "all caught up."

I feel terrible for her because she is all caught up—in a life that she likely saw no possibility of escaping.

She eyes my cigarettes again and I'm happy to give her yet another one if it means we get to keep talking.

## Marked and Trapped

I point to a tattoo on her forearm, a signature of Randy, "Tell me about that."

She looks down and quietly says, "My love," but the way she says it makes me think her "love" is like all of the other "loves" in her life: just another pimp. You see, many times a pimp will tattoo his name onto his "property," like a brand. Sometimes these markings are subtle, but in Tabitha's case, Randy's marking was blatant.

"I see. What about your dreams? What do you wish you could do?" Has anyone ever asked her that? After a few quizzical looks as if to say, "You really want to know?" Tabitha opens up.

"I'd like to go back to school and become an interior designer. I'd like to take people's homes and clean up the inside and add my own personal touches with specific furniture, curtains, carpet, and paint. And I want to move back to Philly so I can take care of my little sister."

"When are you going to do all that?"

"I dunno. I don't think I can. My boyfriend needs me. He even told me once that if I ever left him, he might kill himself."

I don't know what to say to that. Trying to rationalize with her seems inconsequential. When we met, Tabitha was thirty-five and she'd been a prostitute since she was fifteen.

It really was all she'd ever known. She'd been trained from a very young age that survival equals selling your body. I think many people believe that prostitutes want to be in that profession, but the reality is that most of them are trapped into that profession. Tabitha was torn between what she wanted to do and what she was told to do.

During that first meeting, we talked for three hours. I witnessed to her, and I'm convinced God was gracious to use me to speak truth and love into her absurdly hard life.

Over my six days in New York City, I saw Tabitha two more times. On our second meeting, she seemed strung out on some form of methamphetamine. Her bodily contortions seemed demonic. I tried to talk with her, but she was in a hurry and felt like someone was coming after her. She asked if I wanted to sleep with her so she could get money for a bus ticket. Respectfully, I declined the offer and asked if I could pray for her. She yelled no and ran off.

At our last chance encounter, she was more stable, but she'd been crying. She wouldn't tell me why. As we walked down the street, an older man in a fuzzy, leopard-print suit with a gray fedora and alligator-skin boots abruptly pulled her aside. He sported more chain necklaces than a jewelry store. Hollywood couldn't have dressed a pimp any better.

As he held her by the arm, I saw her try to pull away, but she gave into his charm and submitted to what he was saying. I couldn't hear the conversation very well, but I picked up, "Where have you been? What can I do to help? We will get you a bus ticket soon enough. I need you to do this for me."

She eventually returned to me and acted as if nothing had just happened.

I asked, "Who was that?" as if I didn't already know.

She didn't reply.

"C'mon. Who was that?"

"My . . . agent."

I just nodded my head. "Well, okay. How about you tell me about your dreams again? I like hearing about that. Like, what would you do if I hired you to remodel my living room?"

She smiled, then launched into more than a few wild ideas (none of which involved leopard-print, thankfully).

Because of her line of work, I knew she didn't have many men who showed any interest in who she was as a person. They were only interested in her body, and she knew that. When I took the time to get to know her heart, she didn't really know how to react or what to say. All I could do was be there for her and show an interest in who she was as a person rather than as a commodity.

As she dreamed, I prayed, *God, mark her for You someday.*

## The Great Omission

After my experiences with Tabitha, I realized that I needed to rethink my approach to ministering to victims of sex trafficking—and people in general. Though my meetings with her were certainly God-ordained, and I know I was there at that time and in that place for a reason, I couldn't shake the feeling that I was still doing something wrong.

Ministering to the victims of sex trafficking required something more than what I could give on that tour: intentional consistency. Though I was able to show Christ to her on a few occasions, she needed someone who could do that with her on many occasions, over and over again, until Christ could break through her thoroughly protected yet broken heart. Even after that, she would need the consistent, unconditional love of Christ and a Christian community to help her truly break free.

I feared that such inconsistent Christian love would make it seem as if Christ were just like every other man in her life: there one day and gone the next. To fully and effectively minister to sex trafficking victims, Christians need to stop neglecting the necessity of consistently meeting with them. If I say that I'm going to do street ministry at 6 a.m. every Tuesday, then I better be there at 6 a.m. every Tuesday. Even if it falls on Christmas, I show up. These men and women need to know that even though so many of the people in their lives have bailed on them, Jesus Christ never will.

Just consider how different the world would be if Christians remained in the hard places. I fully believe that Tabitha could be freed from her life if Christians faithfully ministered to her every week.

We're supposed to kiss the lions of our culture, as I like to say. We shouldn't fear them. Rather, with faith, we ought to draw near to them.

Christ called us to the Great Commission (Matt 28:18-20). But many Christians like to fallow what I call the Great Omission, where they only interact with people they feel comfortable with. Where they omit the kinds of people in our society who are considered less desirable.

I'd love to one-day walk into a church filled with ex-porn stars, ex-pimps, ex-gang members, and ex-drug dealers. I'd want to walk into a church like that because I'd know that's exactly the kind of church Christ desires. I'd know that the Christians in that room had lived out God's Great Commission.

I know we could all do better at this if we just remember one simple fact: we were all lions to God at one point in our lives.

I find it helpful, when tempted to cast judgment upon people we met, to recall what God tells us in James 2:8–9 and later in verse 13:

> *⁸ If you really fulfill the royal law according to the Scripture, "You shall love your neighbor as yourself," you are doing well. ⁹But if you show partiality, you are committing sin and are convicted by the law as transgressors.*

*[13]For judgment is without mercy to one who has shown no mercy. Mercy triumphs over judgment.*

As far as I know, Tabitha was still on the streets. I continue to pray that God will place a godly man or woman in her life who will be intentional and consistent. I pray that she'll be able to tell me an incredible story of redemption should we ever meet again, whether in this life or the next.

*Many victims are marked by their captor. This isn't always a sure sign, but a possible indication.*

# Journal Entry:
# Beneath the Surface

Day 298 – Arizona

## February 10, 2016

It is funny to me, I have become so focused yet drained at the same time that when I am speaking to new people about either sex trafficking or Jesus, I am on autopilot. I have hit a wall because every single day I am meeting new people who want to hear about what I am doing, which for them is something new and exciting in their normal routine life. But for me each day is filled with new people, places, smells, and a place to lay my head. I am stuck in a twilight zone of having the same conversations with different people because human nature is not to know the person, but their achievements.

Don't get me wrong, I love educating people on this horror that plagues our culture; all I am saying is that my cup is not being filled. The conversations keep hitting a ceiling because the time I have with these new faces is limited. There is no continual fellowship in my life. Even my board members, who are back home, and keep me accountable, can't really comprehend what it is that I am experiencing on a day-to-day basis. Now I know why we are called to go out in sets of two.

I often ask myself what this trip would look like if I had someone else to bike with me throughout it all. Would the impact be greater, or less effective? Would I have met the same people? Would my emotional and spiritual state of mind be different? Would my relationship with Jesus be as close as it is now? Would our media coverage be more or less? Would my plans for after this trip be the same? This is part of my battle, trying to figure out if I really am maxing my full potential or hindering it. I do know that what ever does come of this, God will use it for His glory.

Part of it is also that I can't let anyone know the struggles I am facing. On one side of the coin I need to put on a good face so that people will be happy and encouraged to join the movement to end Human Trafficking, and not become depressed because I told them my sob stories. While on the other side of the coin many times people simply don't care about other people's problems so I don't even try.

We don't take the time to get to know people. Let me ask you this, if a stranger walked into your home and started dumping his or her problems onto you what would your response honestly be? Reading this you may say, "I would listen and try to help!" Well, I hope you would. But the reality is that most often (and I have experienced this more times than not) people will glaze over and not care.

It goes back to my 'Hi how are you' theory. Every time I hear this question posed to me in a greeting I wonder if the person making the statement really wants to know. Sometimes I will even tell a complete stranger how I actually am doing and you know what their response is? They are taken off guard, spell bound and confused that I would tell them how I really am doing.

My theory is that we are culturally programmed to respond with being fine or well. The person asking the question doesn't really care how we are doing because we are innately selfish. We are so consumed with our own problems and worries that we disregard anyone else's problems. We tell ourselves that our struggles far outweigh other people's, and we shut out the world, including our friends and family, diving deep into our self-pity. This eventually can turn into anger, depression, absent mindedness, and/or fear.

I would love to see a culture where we ask the question, "How are you really doing?", and take the time to listen. We can't be afraid to go deeper with someone and get to the root of things. We need to be willing to go beyond the surface level questions and actually dive deep into the heart of things. Yes, that means with complete strangers as well.

I will tell you this from experience through these travels and being placed under different people's roofs almost every night, that if you want to get to the heart of things then get right to it! If the conversation starts out dull, then many times it will stay dull. You have to pose unique and deeper questions within the first 20-30 minutes of being with someone or it won't go much deeper than surface level. Now this is more for people who are strangers, but isn't everyone a stranger if we don't know their heart? Someone who has been in your life for a long time can still be a stranger if you don't know what's beneath the surface.

Word out,
Daniel

# Happy Birthday Sparrow

*"My birthday has always been surrounded by friends and family. I can't image a birthday all alone, let alone being sold to strangers for sex. Heck, not just someone's birthday, but also Christmas, 4<sup>th</sup> of July, Thanksgiving, and any other holiday out there. People are being sold during a time that should be filled with so much joy."*

~Daniel Lemke (journal entry)

Day 135 - Virginia

## September 6, 2015

By this point, I've been on my bicycle for 134 days and have traveled a little over four thousand miles. I'm heading south down the eastern coast of the United States. The leaves on the trees are changing colors, the Blue Ridge Mountains have a majestic presence, and the humidity in the air makes it feel like I am swimming.

When I arrive in Lynchburg, Virginia, I'd planned to stay for five days and go to Liberty University to speak with some of the students and faculty.

I wanted to make the best of my time while I was there and my host had suggested talking with one of the local anti-sex-trafficking organizations called Freedom424. I reached out to them and a couple of other local organizations fighting sex trafficking. A day later, I got a call back from an organization called Homestead Ranch who said they wanted to meet up. I went to dinner with them that evening.

Homestead Ranch is a nonprofit organization that provides safe living spaces for Sparrows. Their safe home had opened its doors just weeks prior to my arrival. Similar safe homes exist across the country and have anywhere from two to forty-eight available beds. Some are only for short-term living situations, and a handful house their survivors for up to seven years.

The 2013, *National Survey of Residential Programs for Victims of Sex Trafficking,* "Of the 37 residential programs that were operational, there were a total of 682 beds exclusively for trafficking victims, 178 for adults, 438 for minors, and 66 for either minors or adults." That number is likely a best guess on available data, as many of these types of homes exist incognito for the safety of their inhabitants. But even this statistic ought to make it clear that we need more homes for kids freed from sex trafficking.[12]

Granted, it's difficult to keep these victims in a safe house for long because it costs a lot: food, specialized treatment (e.g., drug addiction therapy), employee's salaries, the building, insurance, and the grounds that the facility is on. It's a hard number to calculate because there are so many factors that play a role.

For instance, when a nonprofit accepts money from the government, the government can sometimes dictate how that money is used. For a nonprofit like Homestead Ranch, this translates into the government having the power to refuse specific help for victims, add unnecessary programs, move Sparrows around at will, and make the organization do things that aren't beneficial for the Sparrow.

In Homestead's case, they were trying to solve the issue of the government's ability to move Sparrows at their whim. For example, if a Sparrow lived at Homestead for two months and the house was full, but the government wanted to place a new Sparrow in their home, the Sparrow who has only been there two months would be forced to leave—whether or not the Sparrow had made enough progress to leave and maintain a healthy life.

They also have to process how the Sparrows are initially brought into Homestead Ranch. When a Sparrow is picked up after having been rescued they're often placed in jail. Sometimes that's for their own safety, but it's often because they've been charged with prostitution. Once released, they're placed in halfway homes, safe day homes, churches, or temporary places like Homestead Ranch. Each safe home has to figure out the right place for rescued victims so they can comfortable adjust into that safe home. If a safe home can't take in a Sparrow, then many times, the Sparrow goes back to the streets and winds up, "back on the track," a phrase prostitutes use to refer to where they walk and pick up clients.

When I met with Homestead, they had just received government funding and were trying to work through these issues, as well as their additional donor funding. I learned a lot about their uphill battles and we talked well into the night.

Eventually, Kathy, an employee and care provider at Homestead Ranch, asked if I wanted to come to a birthday party they were hosting for one of the Sparrows in two days. "Come to church with us tomorrow.

Afterward, we're having a BBQ and you can meet her. Then on Monday we'll celebrate her birthday."

I was stoked to join them. I couldn't wait to hang out with all of them again and meet the Nadia.

## Sparrow in the Pew

On the next day, I met the founders of Homestead Ranch at their church. A beautiful, twenty-year-old, bronzed skin girl with jet-black hair and wandering eyes sat with them. Nadia was extremely quiet and almost always looked at her feet. When she was asked a question, it would take her a minimum of thirty seconds to respond. Sometimes her response would only be a word or two if she even responded at all. I knew that a lot of that must have come from her past and the abuse she was put through. During church, all I could think to do was continuously pray for her. After the service, Kathy said that was the best behaved that Nadia had ever been in church. Normally, she was fidgety and would often blurt out insults, closely followed by profanities.

After church, I asked Kathy about Nadia's story. I learned that she had been trafficked by her mother and older sister when she was six years old. Nadia had been sexually abused prior to that as well. One reason she doesn't talk much is that her johns would enter her room and beat her if she talked. Often, she would have close to twenty johns in one day.

Nadia came into the care of Homestead Ranch through a missionary who had rescued her from her family about six months prior to my arrival. Before the home was built, she had stayed at Kathy's house because there hadn't been anywhere else for her to go.

Kathy told me of the multiple times they would walk through Costco together. As they'd pass an older man, Nadia's instincts would kick in and she'd ask, "Want me to suck your dick?" The man would be taken off guard and Kathy would pull her aside, reminding her she didn't have to do that anymore.

## Fighting the Demon of Sex Trafficking

Nadia grew up in a culture where Voodoo was the main religion, but it was also mixed with Rastafarianism. Nadia would come to Kathy saying that Rasta (also called *Jah*, the god from Rastafarianism with proclaimed similar roots to Christianity) was controlling her and telling her to hurt someone. Often, the spirit of Rasta would be a perverted version of Mother Mary, whom she would simply call Mary.

Rasta was a demon inside her that would control her by telling her what to do. When I was with Kathy and Nadia, I witnessed a physical change in Nadia's personality and even in the tone of her voice when Rasta would speak.

While Kathy I were talking in the living room after church, Nadia had gone to her room. A couple of hours passed and she came sprinting out of her room, enraged and flailing her arms around in wild punching motions. Her eyes no longer wandered as before. Rather, this time they were large, sharp, and dark. Her head was held high and her voice was loud and booming with anger.

She kept saying she was going to hurt Kathy and that Rasta was telling her to stab her. The normally quiet girl became extremely loud and aggressive while saying, "Rasta is talking now." Then she spewed profanities as her eyes rolled to the back of her head. Nadia's entire body was stiff and her mouth kept twitching. All we could do was battle with prayer.

Spiritual warfare is a very real thing; however, if you haven't experienced it then I would expect you to be skeptical of what I'm

109

saying. But let me put it this way: we believe in things we can't see all the time.

A couple minutes had passed since Nadia flew out of her room. The only way I know how to fight a demon is with the Holy Spirit. When Nadia originally came into the room, I could sense the presence of the enemy.

My discernment flags were going crazy.

At that moment, I prayed quietly to myself so that I would not disrupt the way Kathy preferred to handle this situation. The best way I can describe what happened next, after Nadia said that Rasta was talking, is that her head seemed to pivot almost 180 degrees. Even though her eyes had rolled to the back of her head I still felt as if she were looking right at me.

I believe that Rasta became aware of my praying and felt threatened. Nadia started to yell in a different language that almost sounded like gibberish with a slight slur and interruptive gasps for air.

Without thinking, I jumped to my feet and threw my hands to my side with my palms open and facing outwards. I stared straight into the whites of her eyes and proclaimed Jesus's name. She aggressively approached me, yet could not touch me. It was as if I had a force field in front of me. Kathy, her husband, and a couple of other people surrounded Nadia and started proclaiming the name of Jesus and renouncing Rasta and his companion Mary. As Nadia swayed back and forth, her body contorting in a way I didn't even know the body could move, we continued to pray louder and louder.

It felt like an hour had passed, and maybe it did. I wasn't paying attention to the clock, but our bodies had become exhausted and our

110

spirits were almost all drained.

Nadia suddenly collapsed to the floor. It felt as if a three-hundred-pound man on my shoulders had just jumped off. Kathy rushed to cradle Nadia saying that everything was going to be okay.

Nadia's eyes returned to their normal, bright greenness. Her body limbered up. Yet she had no realization of what had happened over the last two hours.

The room was silent, yet peaceful, as we sat there dazed for a short while trying to process what had just happened. Since it was getting late in the evening and we had much to do over the next two days, I snuck out the back door and rode to my host home.

## Love Bears All Things

The next day, about thirty people showed up to Kathy's house for a BBQ and to celebrate Nadia's twentieth birthday. She'd never had a single birthday party before or had even been recognized on her birthday. On that day, I saw Nadia as the girl God intended her to be. She was filled with joy and even though she reserved her laugh, and her voice was not much louder than a mouse's, I could tell she was happy. I knew the demons in her life were not all gone, but for now, for this day, she was Nadia, not Rasta.

As we gathered in the kitchen around bags of chips, baked goods, grilled hotdogs, and hamburgers, the room went silent as Nadia stared at her very first birthday cake with twenty lit candles dug deep into the frosting. She was wearing a pretty blue shirt and had a birthday crown placed on top her head. Kathy asked her if there was anything she'd like to say.

With a single tear emerging from each eye, she remained silent. A minute passed, then Kathy started to sing: "Happy birthday to you, happy birthday to you. Happy birthday, dear Nadia. We love you. Happy birthday to you!" Not a single eye was dry as Nadia individually blew out each candle with twenty delicate puffs of breath.

When it comes to rehabilitating a Sparrow, you have to be extremely patient and willing to put everything aside. The power of intentional love is what will conquer all. When I think about meeting Nadia and the patient, kind, loving work that Kathy and the Homestead Ranch are doing, I think about 1 Corinthians 13:1–13:

> If I speak in the tongues of men and of angels, but have not love, I am a noisy gong or a clanging cymbal. And if I have prophetic powers, and understand all mysteries and all knowledge, and if I have all faith, so as to remove mountains, but have not love, I am nothing. If I give away all I have, and if I

deliver up my body to be burned, but have not love, I gain nothing.

Love is patient and kind; love does not envy or boast; it is not arrogant or rude. It does not insist on its own way; it is not irritable or resentful; it does not rejoice at wrongdoing, but rejoices with the truth. Love bears all things, believes all things, hopes all things, endures all things.

Love never ends. As for prophecies, they will pass away; as for tongues, they will cease; as for knowledge, it will pass away. For we know in part and we prophesy in part, but when the perfect comes, the partial will pass away. When I was a child, I spoke like a child, I thought like a child, I reasoned like a child. When I became a man, I gave up childish ways. For now we see in a mirror dimly, but then face to face. Now I know in part; then I shall know fully, even as I have been fully known. So now faith, hope, and love abide, these three; but the greatest of these is love.

# Sandwiches of Opportunity

*"One day I will own my own sandwich shop. The only downside is that I would be the most frequent customer, and I would have to give my favorite customers a large discount."*

~ Daniel Lemke (journal entry)

Day 154 - Georgia

**September 19, 2015**

I'd spent a long day riding into my twenty-second state, Georgia. Once again, I didn't have a place to sleep for the night and no real plans other than to hold my head up high and trudge on. Georgia is a beautiful state and I was close to its coast. I left from a family of missionaries in the Marines in Beaufort, South Carolina, whom I got connected with by calling about a dozen churches the previous day. One of the churches reached out to them and they then reached out to me. It took me a long time to leave their house because we had a large breakfast and when I went out to my bike, the rear tire was deflated, again. By the time I replaced the tube it was about 1 p.m.

But this late start would prove to come in handy.

My destination for the day was Savannah, GA. Now, if you've never been there before, imagine two circles within each other. The outer circle of Savannah is dirty, run-down, raided with drugs, and overrun with the homeless. The inner circle is high-class and filled with tourists. It was one of the more drastic distinctions between class systems I'd seen—aside from New Orleans, Portland, and Butte, Montana.

As I pull into Savannah, I'm not in the mood to deal with the world's problems, so I go to what I know best: food. I look up local sandwich shops and start pedaling in one direction, but almost immediately I'm prompted by the Holy Spirit to turn around and go to a sandwich shop that's farther away. Too tired to argue, I pedal that direction. At the restaurant, I take off my helmet and glove and set up my bike in preparation for a feast. Then a man who seems intrigued by my bike approaches me.

"Can't help but to notice your bike. That's a nice ride."

"Thanks."

"What brings you to Savannah on a bike?"

With such a softball of a question, I'm more than ready to hit it out of the park. I tell this stranger about my tour and the work I'm doing to raise awareness about the epidemic of sex trafficking. When I'm done with my well-rehearsed speech, I ask, "What are you doing in Savannah?"

The man smiles. "I'm here for a pastor's conference with Covenant Church!" No way! I grew up going to a Covenant Camp in Estes Park, Colorado."

"Wow. Small world. Do you know a guy named Jesse?"

"Yes! Jesse! He's awesome!"

115

As evidenced by my exclamation marks, we may have had a schoolgirl freak-out moment over knowing the same guy. We talked a little more until my new pastor friend had to leave.

"My name's Garth. It was nice to meet you—"

"Daniel. I'm Daniel. Nice to meet you too Pastor Garth."

I walk into the sandwich shop amazed at how small the world really is. Then I hear the door open behind me and see Garth leaning in.

"We're all gathering together for dinner if you'd like to join us."

I never turn down an opportunity to eat. "Yes. Thank you. Of course. But I'll still be wearing my sweaty biking outfit. It's all I have right now. I travel light."

"Doesn't matter. Come as you are, right? Just meet us at Belfords in an hour."

"Will do. Thanks, Pastor Garth."

I leave the cafe without eating and wander around Savannah wasting time doing one of my favorite things: people-watching.

At the restaurant, I quickly realize I'm very much under-dressed. The entire dining area is filled with people in business-casual outfits. Before I can turn around and bail, Garth thumps me on the shoulder and announces his joy that I'd come. We walk into the establishment and come to a very long table with about twenty-five or thirty people all dressed to the nines. Garth pulls a chair from the middle of the rectangular table and tells me to sit there so everyone can see me better. He sits across from me.

About ten minutes go by and then I ask, "Garth, who are all these people?"

"Oh, we're all the Superintendents of the Covenant Denomination, and over there is the President, Gary Walter." For me, this is like sitting down with the CEO of Apple, Costco, or Home Depot.

I realize that I'm sitting with very important people in my cycling shorts and stinky T-shirt and yet I don't feel judged. In fact, I feel extremely welcomed.

Eventually, Garth has me stand up to give a speech about what I'm doing. I talk for about fifteen minutes to the Superintendents and their wives about my tour and my heart behind ending sex trafficking. When I finish, they all hand me their business cards in order to contact them so I can speak at their churches and find places to sleep more easily.

At that moment, God opened a wide door that would alter the entire course of my tour and eventually shape my path post-tour—but I'll get to that later.

As the feast drew to an end, someone asked if I had a place to stay that night.

I could only tell the truth: "I saw a tent town down the road, so I'm probably going to hang out there."

Gary Walter, the Covenant Denomination President, spoke up, "I'll gladly get you a hotel room for the night, Daniel. But only if you join us in the morning at the church where our conference is taking place and speak to our other members as well."

As I later closed my eyes that night in my own king-sized bed in a paid-for hotel room, I thanked Christ for this opportunity. I prayed, "If it's your will, may even more doors be opened from this encounter."

I'll tell you now: that prayer was answered.

When I think back to my late start on Day 154, the deflated tire that deflated my ego, the decision to follow God's nudge and go to the sandwich shop that was further away. I understand that all of that led up to a divine appointment with a man named Garth, who was willing to talk to a complete stranger in sweaty bicycle shorts.

I want to challenge you to be bold and get outside of your comfort zone to talk with a stranger. You have no idea how it will affect that person and possibly change his or her life forever... Or yours.

# Porn is Cheating

*"We live in a strange day in which there is a rally cry to end sex trafficking, but everybody thinks pornography is okay. Do you see the disjoint in that? Can we not see that one fuels and feeds the other in ways that are heartbreaking? We say we have to end sex trafficking, we have to end the sex trade, yet pornography is accessible on all of our devices and is almost not embarrassing anymore. This is what happens. Ingenuity moves on, but the human soul is stuck and broken, and ingenuity is a good thing, but it numbs us from seeing, 'Hey, something is not right here.'"* [14]

– Matt Chandler, the Village Church

Day 380 - California

## April 27, 2016

How does porn fuel sex trafficking? How are they one and the same? Let me tell you about a guy I met who worked in the porn industry.

While I was in California, I stayed in a house where my host proclaimed himself a Skinhead. Martin was indeed a radical human being. He was outspoken and opinionated about how much America sucks and that socialism is the only way to live. Even though he lived in his trailer-park home with his parents and, as far as I know, is currently unemployed and spends his financial aid money on weed.

Now, I don't really know what got us on the topic of pornography, but I bluntly stated my thoughts: "Pornography is sex trafficking." I went on to talk about a study I had read that had gathered a large group of convicted johns to ask them how many had looked at or were addicted to porn previous to their conviction. A vast majority stated that they were currently or had been addicted to porn. The very small percentage that remained stated that their parents were addicted and it didn't intrigue them personally. A second question asked if the johns had been sexually abused as children. Almost half said yes.

With his boisterous voice, Martin interrupted me and proclaimed, "There are plenty of legitimate porn companies, and the porn industry can't control what the viewer does afterwards."

Now, I'm not claiming that a person who looks at porn will become a predator, or that 100 percent of the porn industry is sex trafficking. However, I am claiming that sex trafficking and pornography are related and both can fuel each other. Just like not all strip clubs are sex trafficking arenas, not all porn is related to sex trafficking either. But I will make the claim that a majority of predators have been affected by the porn industry.

Martin went on to tell me about the punk band he was in, how they'd film the band members having sex, and then sell their videos to porn sites.

My brain automatically identified that as sex trafficking because selling sex took place. However, by definition, this is not sex trafficking. According to Martin's story, the people being filmed were willing. They also thought it would be funny while helping them make easy money. In Martin's eyes, producing porn was a fast way to have fun and earn some dough.

He believed, "Since everyone looks at porn, it isn't harming anyone. And since my porn is clean porn (meaning that no one was doing it against his or her will and/or there was no fraud, coercion, or force), I'm not directly harming anyone."

I refuted his point. "The porn sites you're selling to are directly harming people by helping to fund and fuel the demand for sex trafficking."

He didn't know what to say to that.

As we dove deeper, the truth about one of his band members came out. Her older brother had raped her at a very young age. She then turned to drugs and the punk scene as an escape. In her mind, having sex on film was all right. She'd found her identity in sex. That's how she defined her self-worth.

I've heard extreme feminists state that pornography and strip clubs are an empowerment to women. Maybe the band members thought of producing porn as a form of empowerment.

Let's say that porn is a form of empowerment; that still doesn't negate that the average age of the sex industry (e.g., porn, strip clubs, and prostitution) worldwide is *twelve to fourteen years old,* which means that a *majority of the people in the industry are predominantly children*.

To me, there's no choice or empowerment taking place.

## Why Does Porn Matter?

Most of us understand why sex trafficking is a bad thing, but very few understand why pornography is damaging. Even less know how sex trafficking and pornography are intricately linked.

Objectification of the human body surrounds us. It's in grocery stores, magazines, billboards, and on television. I want to let people know why pornography destroys relationships, self-worth, sex life, and skews one's view of what love is supposed to be. I want people to know that porn affects not only themselves but also the people around them.

I had the privilege of sitting down with an organization in Tulsa called "The Demand Project" (www.thedemandproject.org). The founder of the organization, Jason Weis, is also a police officer and works alongside government officials to get laws passed that help fight human trafficking. The Demand Project is very tuned in with the problem of pornography and what it does to the human mind and relationships. Jason told me about his line of work and how he sets up fake profiles on child pornography sites to catch predators.

One case that really stuck with me was when he posed as a young girl on a well-known porn sight. After months of talking via the site with a man, this predator wanted to meet up with whom he perceived to be a young girl. The predator's intentions were to marry this fourteen-year-old girl, have babies with her, and then—I couldn't believe this when I heard it, or even now—eventually have sex with their babies.

All of this was written throughout hundreds of emails back and forth between Jason and this man in Florida. When I left Tulsa, Jason was planning to go to Florida to testify against this man in court and hopefully get him behind bars.

After being completely shocked from that story, I dared to ask Jason a question that I didn't really want to know the answer to. "What is the youngest case you've seen?"

"Six days old."

I almost vomited.

He told me more about the story. Be warned: this is the most gruesome story I heard on my tour. The mother had sex with men for money so she could get her heroin fix. She eventually became pregnant. After she had her child, she sold him to a man so she could get more heroin.

I wish I could tell you what was going through that man's mind, but it could have been a number of ridiculously perverted thoughts and psychological issues that led him to rape an infant. The baby died from that. When the baby was delivered to the morgue after being found in a dumpster, the autopsy report described the baby as being ripped in two. The perpetrator was eventually caught and thrown in jail for only two years because of the kiddie porn found on his computer.

## More Porn = More Sex Trafficking

Such a man didn't just wake up one day and decide to have sex with children. Such men and women don't just randomly decide one day to have sex for money. It's a progression.

I fully believe that over time and countless hours of diving deeper into the world of porn, a man or woman will become lost and want more of what they can't have. Porn is one of the biggest, if not the biggest, cause as to why the demand for sex trafficking is so vast. It all starts somewhere.

When someone tries so hard to obtain something they can't have, they eventually want more of it and seek it out in the real world. Over time, simply looking at pictures or videos becomes dull. The virtual reality of it all isn't exhilarating or thrilling enough. That thrill in the real world is; sadomasochism, *Fifty Shades of Grey*, lust, cheating, orgies, perverted talk, degrading the opposite gender, rape, sexual harassment, domestic abuse, sexual abuse, catcalling, one-night stands, hookups, masturbation, and more. When someone submits him or herself to the idol of porn, they soon find themselves bowing to its immense power.

No matter how you spin it, porn is an addiction. Many people think they have control over their porn addiction. They believe they can handle it and that it isn't ruining their lives. But doesn't an alcoholic or drug addict think the same way? Addicts think they have control over their addictions, but they don't. That's what makes them an addict.

Those addicted to porn also think they're not hurting anyone when they look at porn. I can't tell you how many people have told me this. I just want to yell, "You're wrong! Of course you're hurting people!"

When an addict clicks on a porn website, the ads on the site are what pay the host of that site. It's how they make their money so that the producers can continue to make pornography and traffic people into the business. Every time an addict clicks to the next image or video, they're adding to the demand for sex, which then says to the producer that they need to increase the supply.

Where do you think that supply comes from?

No one wakes up and says they want to be a porn-star or a prostitute. Circumstances in that person's life have either placed them there, or they're being forced to be there. When we look at the actors in porn, we never think about who's on the other side of the camera or what their life looks like outside of that two minutes of filming for our selfish pleasure. Pornography is nothing more than a visual celebration of rape and a perverse glorification of the degradation of men, women, and children.

## But It's Harmless, Right?

I want to make this very clear: looking at porn is cheating.

A nonprofit in California, named Without Permission, collects stats on survivors who come into their care. One of their questions is, "Were you forced to be filmed for pornography?" Eighty-nine percent said yes to.

This doesn't mean that 89 percent of all porn is a result of sex trafficking, but it does mean that the majority of victims of sex trafficking have been filmed for porn.

I know of other organizations that ask the same question.

Their answers have been as high as 94 percent and as low as 72 percent. I'll say it again, even though not all the actors who appear in porn are trafficked, the majority of people who are trafficked are forced to be in porn. This fact alone shows how much the porn industry contributes the issue of sex trafficking.

If you still don't believe that porn and trafficking go hand-in-hand, then look up the interview, *Former Porn Star, with* ex-porn star Shelley Luben, who was interviewed by Jonathon Van Maren. Again, a warning: portions of Luben's story are graphic.

## Pornography Kills Love

When someone looks at porn, it stimulates the pleasure center of the brain just like drugs do. It makes the brain more active. Our dopamine receptors become less sensitive to available dopamine, which depletes the sensitivity to the normal pleasure found in any given activity. Just like many things we overexpose ourselves to, we become numb and try to seek out more so we can get that same euphoric thrill we once had when it all started. Porn is a drug, so we need to treat it like a drug. People become dependent on porn, slipping further and further from soft to hardcore and then to child/teen porn. The number one search in porn is teen/young.

Pornography kills love. When we become dependent on porn, it skews our perception of what love really is. It makes us think that love is strictly physical and that we don't have to work at our relationships at all. In porn, people just meet, have sex, and its all fun and games—a fantasy world where people are objects and you can shop from item to item. But in the real world, we have responsibilities. We actually have to work for our relationships, whether that's with family, friends, or a spouse. When a person gets so wrapped up in the fantasy of porn, it makes them think that's how the real world is, but it is not.

A porn addict believes that it's alright to go from person to person because that's how they've trained their minds through switching from profile to profile. This is one reason why the divorce rate has gone up. People don't think they have to work for their relationships anymore. When we view porn, it tells us that we can click to the next profile when they start doing something we as the viewer don't like. We click from one girl to another girl and train ourselves that we can take that to the real world. Maybe our wife messed up and I didn't like it so I'm going to "click" to the next wife. [13]

We become secluded to the world around us, because after facing the reality of not liking what our wife did, we want to revert to the fantasy world. People who view porn often revert to this fantasy world, not only because of their porn addiction but also because they lacked parents who showed them what love and respect really are. It could also

126

be rebellion or peer pressure. Parents need to talk to their children about pornography and how the people in those videos are actually slaves.

## Stopping Sex Trafficking Means Ending Pornography Addiction

We can fight pornography by keeping each other accountable. Don't fear talking about it with each other.

My little brother and I used to talk in code to each other. We wanted to have a secret language. (We were strange kids.) We'd say things like, "A boar only roars once." That would mean we had to go to the bathroom. "The roof on the house is upside-down" was a question if we were lost while exploring.

Maybe you need to make up code words with someone you can hold yourself accountable to, to make it easier to talk about a porn addiction. For example, "Did you see the hummingbirds?" Whatever your phrases are, your code is meant to make it easier to keep each other accountable. If I'm helping someone struggling with a meth addiction, I'm not going to ask them in a crowd of people how they're doing with their meth addiction. It puts them on the spot and could make them not want to tell you. But, if you use a code, then it can be discussed as soon as you think about it, whether that's in public or private, and it won't make either party feel uncomfortable. When it pops into your mind, discuss it then so you won't forget to bring it up later.

I suggest finding an accountability partner who isn't your peer. Choose someone who's older. Chances are they've gone through it, have overcome it, and are more likely to be able to give you wisdom. We can't have the blind leading the blind.

Also, when people have their peers as accountability partners, they tend to brush it off much more easily rather than diving deeper into the root of the problem. They say, "Oh yeah, I struggled this week too," and nothing else is said. Accountability is key because only together can we break the cycle.

Sometimes extreme measures are necessary. I think of part of Jesus's Sermon on the Mount:

> You have heard that it was said, "You shall not commit adultery." But I tell you that anyone who looks at a woman lustfully has already committed adultery with her in his heart. If your right eye causes you to stumble, gouge it out and throw it away. It is better for you to lose one part of your body than for your whole body to be thrown into hell. And if your right hand causes you to stumble, cut it off and throw it away. It is better for you to lose one part of your body than for your whole body to go into hell. (Matthew 5:27–30)

You may need to get rid of your computers, cell phones, and tablets. Go back to flip phones and letters!

Some of us can't really do that, but there are applications like Covenant Eyes (http://www.covenanteyes.com) and XXXChurch (https://www.xxxchurch.com) that help block sites that aren't appropriate and link your computer or phone to your accountability partner. More often than not, it takes extreme measures to get rid of extreme circumstances.

The biggest lies Satan tells us about consuming porn is that we're the only ones who struggle with it, that people will judge us, and that we're weak if we have problems with it. Don't let Satan control your life. Seek help. Don't let him destroy your self-worth and love.

Looking at another human being through your screen is cheating. (Matt 5:28)

We're in this together, and it may just be our greatest step toward ending sex trafficking.

# Journal Entry:

# Beauty in the Streets

Day 212 – Louisiana

## November 15, 2015

Aside from the chaos, my host and I got to experience the beauty that is within NOLA. Today, there's a festival downtown. The same wildly dressed locals flood the area. The smell of gumbo and live music fills the air. I don't believe I've ever had such tasty food in my life.

We sit in the grass field talking about NOLA's history and culture. I turn the conversation by talking about the history of sex trafficking. They light up and tell me that tomorrow we can go to church and they'll have me speak to their congregation.

The following day, we drive to the part of NOLA that I'd refer to as the ghetto.

My mind was totally at peace, I couldn't wait to hear the pastor and speak to the congregation.

We arrive at a brown brick building that's gated off.

"I believe it used to be an old school building," my host assures me.

As we drive to the back, I notice the basketball court and a handful of windows that have been boarded up.

My host runs the coffee bar at the church, which means we get to talk with most of the congregation face-to-face. I love seeing Christ working through people and hearing the stories he's placed over their lives.

This church has all kinds of people: ex-drug lords, homeless, abused, divorced, sick, formerly imprisoned, and the list goes on. I could have listened to each person's story for hours.

It's a tightly packed room with roaring music. The pastor makes several jokes during announcements. His personality fills the room with joy.

"Today, we have a special guest. Now, many of you might think he's crazy, but I just had coffee with him . . . and you're right!"

The room bellows with laughter as he continues. "I do believe that he is seven months into his journey by now. Hey, Daniel! Are your thighs just giant rock boulders now?"

As I thump my legs I say, "Another couple months, they'll be iron."

"I bet they will be! Now, Daniel, I would like for you to share with our church what it is that you are doing."

I pause for a couple of seconds to allow for the dynamic of the room to change slightly. I didn't want the laughter to die so abruptly. But as I start to feel all the eyes in the room shift toward me, I tell them all about my mission.

"I'm riding my bicycle circumferencing the United States for fifteen months. I'm riding to raise awareness about domestic sex trafficking."

I keep the conversation brief and end with an invitation to speak with me after church.

I'm so thankful that Christ put me in that church so that I could experience how He has each of His children and to see His love for each and every one of them.

Love,
Daniel

# Death's Doormat

*"I've always found that anything worth achieving will always have obstacles in the way and you've got to have the drive and determination to overcome those obstacles on route to whatever it is that you want to accomplish."*

~Chuck Norris

Day 253 – Texas

## December 27, 2015

I wanted to be able to say I went the entire fifteen months without getting hurt or sent to the hospital. But then I contracted hypothermia—in Texas. I learned that when you're dancing on the doormat of death's house, you're teasing a beast whose rage isn't forgiving; it's only provoked.

## Freezing in Texas

After church on December 27, I venture out from Copper Canyon, Texas toward Weatherford. The temperature is 44° as a light drizzle descends. I know it's not going to be a tremendously fun ride, but I want to stay on schedule and get to my next speaking engagement. Up until this point, I've kept on schedule and made it to every single city I've set out for. I haven't accepted a single ride from anyone. I'm determined to ride my bicycle the entire tour.

About seven miles into this Texas ride, the rain starts pounding and a fourteen-mile-per-hour crosswind begins to blow. It's a full-on monsoon. The temperature eventually drops to 36°, causing the rain to mix with the wind. Pellets of ice bounce off my face and body like a swarm of hornets attacking an intruder.

This is not my brightest moment in life: I'm also riding in only my rain jacket and biking shorts, because the day before was 78°! Texans call this drastic temperature change a "Blue Northern."

Within an hour of riding, my waterproof jacket is soaked all the way through. I'm a moving Popsicle. I'm reminded of the scene in *The Wizard of OZ* where the Tin Man is stuck because he doesn't have any oil in his joints. My body struggles to function and starts shutting down. My mind creaks, *Oil! Oil! Oil!*

I'm supposed to travel sixty-four miles today, a relatively easy day for me. But when my body shuts down and prohibits me from biking any faster than nine miles per hour downhill, I know I'm in trouble. However, my pride is still set on completing the day. In my mind, if I don't complete it then I've failed. I wanted the title of going fifteen months without a single ride while keeping on schedule.

## Pops to the Rescue

About forty-eight miles into the ride, I call the gentleman who's putting me up in a hotel that night to let him know what's going on. Everyone calls him "Pops."

"Pops, I'm about seventeen miles away from you, but I'm not sure I'll be able to make it to you. I'm freezing and moving slow."

"Sorry to hear that, Daniel. I can come pick you up. Just tell me what road you're on." Prideful, and still not wanting to relinquish my goal, I say, "Thank you, but not yet. Lemme see how much farther I can go. Seventeen miles isn't that far for me." We hang up.

Ten minutes later I call again.

"Pops—"

"I'm on my way, Daniel. Hang in there."

As I wait by the side of the road, I'm in so much pain that my vision begins failing. My body's so stiff that every time I move, it feels like my muscles are ripping in half. My bones feel like knives digging into my joints. My spoken words aren't audible.

Pops arrives and drives me to the hotel. In his car, my body feels like it's on fire. It doesn't feel like the heat of fire—more like the burn that's left afterward, and I feel that way over my entire body.

I immediately drink two hot cups of coffee at the hotel and jump into a hot shower in my first-floor room. I'm uncontrollably screaming, yelling, and crying so loudly that I'm sure people on the third floor can hear me.

## What It Feels Like When Your Body Freezes Over

You know that feeling you get when you put a tight rubber band around your finger and all the pressure builds up in the tip? Well, take that feeling and put it all over your body. You know that painful tingling you get when your ligaments are waking up after sleeping on it wrong? Times that by six. Add a perpetual state of tunnel vision and walking the fine line between consciousness and passing out. Oh, and don't forget feeling like you're on fire.

I can barely make a coherent sentence. I have almost no control over any of my motor functions.

Let me put it this way: I've broken a lot of bones and have had many stitches throughout my life. I would much rather endure the pain of breaking both arms and all of my fingers at the same time than endure hypothermia again.

I stand in the shower with the water turned all the way on hot. I can barely feel it. I spend thirty minutes in the shower trying to warm up my body. Again, my pride gets the best of me because I don't want to go to the hospital. "Being cold" seems to be the absolute lamest reason to go.

Before that point, the only times I'd gone to the hospital – which I frequently visited when I was younger—were for broken bones, stitches, or my appendectomy. Heck, I wouldn't even see a doctor for being sick. The only time I was around doctors was if I couldn't fix it myself.

But for this situation, I soon realized that I had to set aside my pride and let Pops take me to the hospital. When I arrive at the hospital, I stumble up to the front desk, attempt to tell the receptionist my situation (I still can't make a coherent sentence), and then I promptly fall to the ground because my legs give out. They grab a wheelchair, set me in it, and take my vitals.

Keep in mind that I'd just taken a thirty-minute, fully hot shower and I'd had three cups of hot coffee by this point. When the nurse took my temp, it was 96.2° hypothermia sets in at 95°. My blood pressure is 154 over 72, which is actually pretty good and to be expected with all the bicycling I did. My heart rate is 58 beats per minute, also very good.

135

Basically, my vitals are all normal except that my temp is far too low. They immediately hook me up to an IV, take my blood to test for organ damage, and then start pumping a warm saline solution into my veins to warm me up from the inside out.

When your body experiences hypothermia, your core temperature drops below the threshold where your organs can function well. Most of your blood is pulled away from your extremities to keep your core warm. Specific organs then each release a certain protein that will show up in the blood. The doctors can analyze that protein to determine which organs are damaged. This is why they tested my blood, but they also had to test if I was on any drugs. Luckily, no other damage had taken place.

## Giving Up

This experience was an extremely humbling situation and a well-learned lesson in letting someone take care of me. The best part is that Pops was a complete stranger to me before and had no idea what he was getting himself into when he offered to put me up for the night. If Pops hadn't been around to take care of me and make sure that I was okay, I might not have made it to tell the tale. But by the grace of Christ, I am still kicking and determined to keep going.

The next day, I wake up extremely sore and very stiff. I have knots on my neck and thighs the size of golf balls. As I peer out from my hotel room window in the morning, I see ten inches of snow on the ground. I know I'm not going to be going anywhere for a little while, so I do the only thing I can do: I give up.

Ha! Not!

By this point in the tour, the only thing that would have stopped me was death itself—which it almost did.

I call Mr. and Mrs. Mathews in Anna, Texas (just north of Dallas) to see if I can stay with them again. I'd stayed with them for Christmas thanks to a dear friend, Sam Moreton, who'd helped me find hosts before I'd even crossed into Texas. He had some friends in the Dallas area who he reached out to in hopes that they'd be willing to host me. The Mathews were beyond gracious to take me in for the holidays. We had never met before but had a mutual friend in Sam.

Once again, little did they know what they were getting themselves into once they agreed to host me.

John Mathews and his boys drive two hours to get me from the hotel and drive me back to his house. The original plan was to have my little brother Jesaja, along with my three best friends, Caleb, Elijah, and Connor, come out and help me get across western Texas. They were going to be a support vehicle, since western Texas is beyond desolate.

While I was in the hospital, they were already preparing to drive out from Colorado to join me for a couple of weeks. However, since my pride had taken me for a ride, our plans had to change.

I had to ask the Mathews family not only if I could come back to their house until the weather got better, but also if four other grown men could come over as well. Once again, the Mathews surprised me. Without hesitation, they were willing to host all of us.

We spent New Year's there and had, what John Mathews refers to as, a "Man Feast," where the only cooked food is meat and the only acceptable vegetable is potato chips. I spent my New Year's eating heaping mounds of meat, worshiping Jesus around a campfire, and spending time with my closest friends and a family. That is the full-blown example of love.

137

# Getting Political

*"Nearly all men can stand adversity, but if you want to test a man's character, give him power."*

~ Abraham Lincoln

Day 259 – Texas

## January 2, 2016

Leaving the Mathews family is heart-wrenching. We had bonded greatly within the couple of weeks I'd spent with them, but I have a mission to live out. Elijah, Caleb, Connor, Jesaja, and I all hop into Elijah's tiny Toyota Corolla and head south to Austin because none of them, beside Connor, had been there before. Our plan is to go on a small adventure then drive to Lubbock to get me back on schedule for my speaking engagements.

Once we arrive in Austin, some of us sleep in the car while others find trees in the hillside to pitch a hammock between and camp out. When we wake up in the morning, we wander around Austin and come across a store solely dedicated to hot sauce.

Once we walk in, we see that one of the hot sauces is locked up in a cage. We ask the guy behind the counter why it's locked up. Without a word, he pulls out a bottle and five toothpicks. The bottle he pulls out is different than the one locked up, but we're intrigued. He opens the bottle, takes the point of the toothpick, and lightly dabs it in the hot sauce. He hands me the toothpick. "Try it."

The toothpick looks clean. I can't even see the sauce. I say, "What the heck?" and lather my tongue with the toothpick. No sooner have I placed it on my tongue, than I'm yelling like a fire-breathing dragon. It's so spicy that my eyes water and I begin to sweat profusely. The gentleman then looks at me and says, "The reason why *that* one is locked up is because it's about four levels *hotter* on the Scoville scale."

Of course, I tell all my friends to try it. Minutes later, we're all dying, regretting everything. I love being a man, partially because we make each other do stupid things.

We spend a couple of days wandering around and filling our time with random shenanigans. Before heading west to Lubbock, we go to The Village Church in the Dallas area where Matt Chandler is the pastor.

## We the People

On a beautiful Sunday in January, we arrive at the home of our host in Lubbock, TX. The following day, we work to make local connections for the cause. All of us head for Yellow House, the local coffee shop. Their wide assortment of delicious gourmet coffee overwhelms me. I tell the barista to make something special, just as long as it's a black cup of coffee! She brings out a delicious pour-over coffee that blows my mind with how fantastic it is. For a black cup of coffee it is sweet, with a note of love that bounces on my tongue.

Throughout the morning, we call churches, edit blogs, and research government officials who we could contact. We call the office of Texas Senator Charles Perry and get an appointment to sit down with him tomorrow.

We're so excited that we call Texas Representative, Dustin Burrows' office as well. To our surprise, he's able to meet with us tomorrow afternoon! We're all so pumped that we hoot and holler and do a little happy dance in our chairs. I'm blown away at how easy it was for us to call a Senator and a Representative and set up appointments. I thought it was going to be weeks out before we'd even get to sit down or that they wouldn't even want to speak with us.

A young lady, about our age, overheard our conversation. She approaches us to figure out what we're all excited for. She introduces herself as Jana and from our conversation we knew this was the beginning of something beautiful.

She's been on several cross-country bicycle tours herself. Immediately, we connect. After a while of talking and hanging out, it's time for us men to get dinner. A couple of hours later, Jana texts me to ask if we want to come over on Wednesday for a game night she's hosting. We tell her we'd love to but can only come for a short time because I have a college group to speak to. However, we could come after that if they were still hanging out.

## Our Political Parties

Our day of meetings is at hand. Senator Perry allows us to open the conversation with prayer. This sets the whole mood of our talk from the very beginning because we are able to speak the same language and have the conversation be Christ lead. We speak about current bills in government that are combating sex trafficking and who's doing what about this situation. We discuss the disconnect in the church and how often a huge detach exists between talking and doing. He brings up a good point: we need to do two things to make the connection between words and actions: one is faith that God can help us fulfill the words we say and put them into action. The other is the desire to live the actions out.

In the afternoon, we meet with Representative Dustin Burrows. Our time with him goes far better than we expected. It begins with me educating Representative Burrows about domestic sex trafficking with the help of Elijah and Caleb. Our discussion triggers his mind to steer the conversation toward the Drug Court system, an alternative method of rehabilitating drug addicts through a strict process of accountability. It gives people who struggled with addictions an alternative to incarceration.

We discuss the possibility of adding survivors of human trafficking to this Drug Court system to help them through the rehabilitation process. Many times, the kids who are trapped in human trafficking are also heavily addicted to drugs. The Drug Court already has programs in place for veterans with PTSD, juveniles, and families. We want to adapt this system to accommodate survivors of sex trafficking. We'd need to add safe housing, proper counselors, funds for relocation, and a system that identifies these people as victims of sex trafficking as opposed to regular offenders. We also need people who are willing to meet victims where they are and understand that a lot of the time will have to be invested in these survivors' lives.

Eventually, Representative Burrows connects us with Judge Reyes, who leads the local Drug Court system, so we can sit in on a Drug Court session that Thursday. We're able to meet with Judge Reyes in the morning, talk about how the Drug Court system works, and get his insight into how he runs things in his Drug Court.

Thursday evening, Jana meets up with us and we sit in on a session with about eighty people or so. Judge Reyes talks to each person face-to-face and engages with them. Judge Reyes knows whether each person has messed up or has been good through the report from their respective caseworkers. If they've been good, they are rewarded with all sorts of things, from gift cards to less parole time. If they have messed up, they are placed with restrictions, such as having to attend more meetings, take more drug tests, or endure community service.

They're punished so that they'll understand that their actions have consequences. While we're there, the Judge also hands out recognitions of encouragement as well as "motivation" for those who've slipped up.

To Judge Reyes, "motivation" means that if they messed up again, they'd be put in jail, but for the time being they only have to prove that they want to be in this program. The way Judge Reyes goes about engaging each person is extremely powerful. His passion and love for each person in the room is very prevalent. It's encouraging to me to see the court system work in such a powerful way.

About an hour into the session, a young child no more than eight years old, who was sitting with his mother, looks up at the Judge as he passes and says, "Thank you for saving my mom's life."

It takes a slow moment for the courtroom to process what the kid's just said. Judge Reyes has the boy repeat himself because the boy had spoken while Judge Reyes was speaking. Hearing the child's thanks, the courtroom burst into tears. It had already been a pretty emotional time because of the encouragement and motivational talks, but that little boy was the icing on the cake.

The Drug Court posed a sense of belonging, instead of condemnation for our offenses. Don't get me wrong: if someone really messed up and didn't want to get help, they'd reap the consequences. But for those who wanted help and moral support, then the Drug Court was the right place for them.

The Drug Court is something you'll have to experience for yourself to experience its power, but brace yourself for crying and seeing hope in the court system. Seeing this system work the way that it does sparks a longing in us to get survivors of sex trafficking into a network like this.

Judge Reyes told that there are a few Drug Courts around the United States that do help victims of sex trafficking in the same way. I have not personally been to one, but would absolutely love the opportunity to visit one.

After the Drug Court ends, we debrief with the Judge and ask some final questions before parting ways. We learn more about the stories of a few specific people in the program.

## Those Who Follow the One Weird Dude

We leave the Drug Court and head to Jana's house for some food and to hang out with some of her friends from the game night. It's four ladies and five guys. Our conversation is extremely fruitful. I've never experienced a group of people being so open and encouraging with each other. We're able to relay how God has gotten us through the good times and the bad. We end up pausing the conversation to go two-stepping at a local country western club because that had been the original plan. I'm really glad that we do so because it allows time for our previous conversations to sink in. We have a blast.

I've grown up not really caring what other people think about me, which allows me to be me and not conform to social norms. So, in this case, when we arrive to see the dance floor pretty barren with the crowd around the perimeter, I go straight to the dance floor and begin dancing like a fool! I notice people pointing and laughing, but I don't care.

My friends are encouraged to join in, which they do, and this helps everyone have a much better time—rather than awkwardly standing on the sidelines. We're all laughing and making great memories.

Eventually, the whole bar is dancing like us! Even some of the cowboys join our "hip-hop" (more hop than hip) dance circle.

At that moment, I realize not only the importance of a leader but the importance of the first two followers. If no one had joined me, I would have just been one weird dude dancing. But as soon as someone else joins that weird dude, others are motivated to join in too. It creates momentum because the one weird dude is no longer the outsider. It reverses the situation and motivates people to join the movement.

I heard a quote that sums it up nicely, "If the leader is the flint, the first follower is the spark that really makes the fire." We need leaders, but their efforts are rendered useless if no one joins them. [15]

Don't ever feel like following is a bad thing. Without followers, no movement would ever happen. It would just be a bunch of people with grand ideas that would fall by the wayside, since no one has joined in with them.

As the night progressed till the stroke of midnight, we take the ladies back home. As soon as we get back to their house, our earlier conversations continue right where they left off, as if there were no interruptions.

However, our conversations dive deeper than before, something I didn't think was possible with people we'd just met. As the sun creeps up on the horizon, we figure we should call it a "night" because all of us would be parting ways in a couple of hours. As we leave, we knew that our newfound friendships would progress into deeply rooted relationships.

*Daniel, Elijah, Connor, Caleb, and Jesaja*

*Daniel and Judge Reyes*

# Journal Entry:

# Pastor Pimp

Day 51 - Illinois

## June, 2015

For me, this story was hard to believe until I got to Springfield, Illinois and met my first survivor of sex trafficking in person. I met April through my host family, who were very involved in the community. They knew my line of work and asked if I would like to meet up with a local organization. I accepted the offer and the next day I was sitting down with April.

At the time I met her, April was forty-two years old and beginning her own anti-sex-trafficking organization. She was creating a safe home for women of domestic violence and sex trafficking. I wanted to know her story and understand why she wanted to help women who had been trafficked.

April was an excellent girl in school, never ditched classes, always did her homework, and wanted to be a nurse when she grew up. After high school, she fell madly in love with a charming man in seminary. A couple of years later, they married. April's new husband became the head pastor of a church while she worked in the trauma unit at a hospital.

To the world around them, their life looked amazing and filled with love. His church congregation was growing. April's patients always loved seeing her smiling face. When they were together, they always seemed to be supportive of each other.

146

But behind the curtain was a completely different story.

I'd guess the problems began with her husband's heavy addiction to pornography. He had tried to get help for it, but the church board kept pushing it aside by saying that they'd pray for him. No action or follow-ups occurred. (Let me make this clear: prayer is necessary in such events. However, if we don't keep a person accountable and get them help when they need it, then we're promoting the sin. It's much easier to ignore a problem, but when we do it allows the issue to fester and grow).

At home, April's husband would film them having sex without her knowledge. Eventually, he wanted to tie her up during sex and their bedroom activities quickly became more and more aggressive. He would twist the meaning of Bible verses to get April to believe that everything they were doing was biblical. It even got to a point where he argued, "It's what God wants" when he brought other people into their bed.

During this time, April was trying to do the right thing, but her husband had her wrapped around his finger. She had no idea she was a victim of sex trafficking—by her own husband and a pastor no less.

April was a victim of sex trafficking because her husband took videos of her without her knowledge, sold them on the Internet for profit, and the other people he had in their bedroom were paying him to be there. Does that mean sex trafficking only occurs when there's an exchange of money? No, April was trafficked because she was being filmed against her will and manipulated to think that what she was doing was right.

While April spoke about her sex life to a good friend, her friend told her how abnormal such a situation was. Once April found out about the filming, she knew she had to do something. She went

147

to the church board and told them what was going on. They denied her complaint and told her that if she ever brought it up again, they'd ruin her reputation. But April was finished being walked all over. April felt empowered and started consciously questioning her home situation.

This time she didn't stop at the church board, but went above their heads to the superintendents of the entire congregation. She brought them the movies of her that she found and told them her story.

Within a matter of hours, her husband was fired and a restraining order was set in place. I wish I could say that he received jail time, but he didn't.

Daniel Lemke

# Movement Creates Friction

*"Everything that moves creates friction."*
~ Bill Bathman

## Tick or Treat

Our website, www.bikethroughtraffic.com, was hacked in October 2015 around Halloween by thirty-two different entities—that we know of.

A couple of unknown entities hacked in and many more followed shortly after, tangling and connecting our anti-sex-trafficking site to many pro-porn sites. They got into my emails and spammed many people on our email list.

Eventually, we were blocked by our servers, which prevented normal viewers from seeing our website. To many who didn't know what Bike Through Traffic was, this wrecked a lot of our organization's credibility. For some reason, people tend to take you more seriously if you have a website. Our donations trickled off and we lost content. People who had our old email address couldn't contact me because my email address was linked to the website.

It was a mess.

However, the battle didn't end there. Once our website went down, many people wrote harsh comments on news articles websites that had been written about me. They said I was on a selfish crusade and spending all the donations on expensive cars and traveling to exotic places. Making comments like; "What an idiot. I could have done this way faster in a car." "Bike Through Traffic is a scam."

I was getting hate mail and I even had a porn star get onto my Facebook page and make sexual comments that were damaging to my reputation, like, "I enjoyed fucking you last night," even though we were seven states apart. However, the people who didn't know where I was questioned the comments and started harassing me. Pastors and friends were getting emails from my email account saying things that didn't really make sense, like "Daniel has died, collect his bounty."

Aside from all the hacking and media-based spiritual attacks, I was struggling with what I was doing and how useless I felt. Was I really making any difference in the world?

This is when I wanted to give up more than I ever had before. (Well, by day four of the tour I'd wanted to give up, and I wanted to quit almost regularly throughout the tour.) At this point, during this attack, I wasn't just thinking of giving up on the tour, I was thinking about giving up on life.

Several times while on tour, I attempted to take my life.

One time, I swerved out into traffic trying to get hit by a passing semi. Yet, each time I tried, I'd throw my head down anticipating the hit but when I brought my head back up, I'd be back on the side of the road.

I even remember a "Frogger" moment as I went straight through a red light with my eyes closed and miraculously missed every single car. Jesus had my back and was with me the whole time, even though I didn't want to be there and thought that I couldn't handle all these attacks.

After the site went down and the digital dust settled, I realized that my trip and my life were truly in the hands of God. I understood that I have no control over anything that may or may not happen.

Jesus had won!

This gave me the opportunity to fully rely on Christ and trust that He would open the correct doors for me to walk through. Before, I had constantly tried to make connections myself, contact the "right" people, and point them toward our website.

After the hacking, more connections happened than before. I spoke to more people in authority and reached much larger audiences, because I was fully relying on Christ.

I learned how hard it is to see God's hand in life when focusing on the problems—or, in my case, the semis—right in front of you.

# Chase The Roar

*"Don't ask to hear the voice of the Lord unless you are prepared to act on it."*

~ Author Unknown

Day 364 – California/ Washington

**April 18, 2016**

I'm at a sandwich shop, again, and I'm sitting down with a pastor. Midway through our lunch a couple of lovely, elderly ladies join us. This restaurant seems to be the city's hot spot. So many of the people from the church I've just spoken at are arriving.

After hearing me speak at the church, these two ladies wanted to know more about my mission and background. So, we talk about sex trafficking and what it looks like locally.

They ask, "How do children get caught up in those situations?" and, "Why aren't the pimps put in jail?" and, "How can we know when sex trafficking is occurring?"

I provide the answers I've provided across the country. To their last question, I say, "We see sex trafficking *every day*, but we've become numb to it. Pornography is everywhere—our grocery stores with the magazines, media and ads, television shows that can't go five sentences without making a sexual joke or reference, the list goes on. Porn and sex trafficking go hand-in-hand. There's a street that every city has—that street where we all know some shady things happen. That street where we know prostitutes and drug dealers are—"

One of the ladies cuts me off. Her story goes something like this: "My husband was driving down a street like that and came to a stop sign and without any exchange of words, a hooker hopped into his car. My husband told her that he wasn't looking for any of that and that she needed to get out of his car. As he was driving home, he called me and said that he's going to need to wash his entire car afterwards."

Fury rises within me, but outwardly I keep my cool. I'm upset that her husband felt as if he needed to wash his car after she got in. I let the conversation go on a little while longer so I can gather my thoughts and have a productive conversation without making this lady feel attacked.

On one side of the coin, I have a reputation to upkeep that says to take a stand for the least of these. But on the other side, I wrestle with the fear of being an outcast, because I didn't find her story humorous. Deep down, I know I can't let this go unnoticed.

But I fear being different and the possibility of offending her.

After a few minutes, a wonderful segue brings the conversation back around to more serious matters. With boldness, confidence, and strategic wording, I ask, "Did you ever think about the opportunity your husband missed out on to witness to that lady? Or were you too caught up in the need to wash your car?"

Now I have my audience. They're all speechless.

I leap on the opportunity to continue my thoughts, "I just don't understand how we can be so quick to judge others, rather than take into consideration the other person's needs or hurts. If we took a couple of minutes out of our days to realize the moments that are smacking us in the face to reach out and put others before ourselves, then we could live in a much better world."

Of course, in the back of my mind, I'm worried about what they'll think of me and that they may not come to my speaking engagement that evening. But, at the same time, I *have* to jump on the opportunity to point out that we—especially as Christians—need to love others before ourselves. We need to jump on every opportunity to share the gospel, whenever we can.

I couldn't sit by and let my elders who confessed to be Christians, speak disrespectfully about another human being.

Then as now, I thought of Matthew 7:13–14:

> "Enter by the narrow gate. For the gate is wide and the way is easy that leads to destruction, and those who enter by it are many. For the gate is narrow and the way is hard that leads to life, and those who find it are few."

Going against society's norms is extremely uncomfortable and possibly the hardest thing I will ever do.

## Into the Lion's Den?

I loved looking for each state's official sign. Every time I knew I was coming into a new state, I could see the state line on my Garmin GPS. However, the "Welcome to State" sign wasn't always where it should be. Sometimes, I'd have to go on a voyage just to find it. Or it'd be in the middle of a highway and I'd have to figure out how to get to it, so I could take my picture with it.

For me, those new state signs were breaths of fresh air. They not only meant I was that much closer to finishing the tour, but they also meant new opportunities—some of which were, how do I say this? Sketchy.

After an ordeal of going too far to take a picture of a Washington state sign on top of a bridge, I finally cross the steel trap and arrive in Kelso, Washington. I'm ready to fill my belly after burning 3,853 calories.

I love sandwiches and almost every time I eat one on the tour, something amazing seems to happen. I head to a local Subway and order my turkey-and-ham sub on honey oat bread. I could have eaten three foot-longs, but I've come to the realization that I'm in a perpetual state of hunger.

In the corner, some high school choir kids are singing off-key while using the subs as microphones. On the side, a police officer sits with his head hung low. Eventually, I thank him for his services and ask how his day's going. The officer says, "It's been a brutal day."

"What's going on, sir?"

"Just got back from a suicide call."

After sympathizing with him, I ask "Do you have a family?" "Two kids and my wife."

"Can you do me a favor? When you get home, love them. Show them how much they mean to you. Also, can I pray for you?"

The officer's face starts to well up with tears. He nods his head and says thanks. He gets back to his work and I get back to my sandwich.

A little while later, another cross-country cyclist comes in the door. Our eyes widen and with a rush of joy overtaking us both, I get out of my chair, run over to him, and hug this complete stranger as if embracing a brother. Yet, he doesn't feel like a stranger because we have the bond of touring. I invite him over to my table to sit with me and chitchat.

Jonah is a French-Canadian with the mission to take on Monsanto, a large scale food corporation. He wants to educate people on how to eat better and what's going into their food. It's fascinating, but I'm just excited to see another tourist come out of hibernation. Jonah's planning on biking another twenty miles into the mountains to camp out for the night.

I'm tempted to join him since I have no plans for where I'll lay my head tonight, but I'm pretty tired and know that my job in Kelso isn't finished.

After an hour of talking, we part ways with the biker's benediction: "May the wind be at your back."

## More than (a) Halfway Home

One of my unspoken side projects on this tour has been trying to figure out the logistics of running a sub shop. How much do you need for product? How much should you charge? Basically, I wanted to know the entire business side of a sandwich shop because one day I'd like to own one and hire survivors of sex trafficking—but I'll get to that later.

After Jonah the Monsanto-fighter left, I talk to the manager, Jacob, of the Subway shop about how many tomatoes and pounds of lettuce they go through each day. Eventually, the conversation steers toward Christ and my mission to help victims get a job.

I feel honored because this guy is soaking up everything. He's extremely courteous and respectful to what I have to say. He keeps going to the back to get rough estimates of his weekly orders to give me a better perspective of what I should be looking for.

Later, we talk about good places to camp out around town where I won't get in trouble or get robbed.

He looks at me and says, "Hold on. Let me go make a call."

Three minutes later, Jacob says, "If you want, we have a ministry home that you can go stay at."

I'm a little taken aback because I didn't know what to expect, but I accept. "Heck yeah!" He hands me the address and phone number of the guy who runs the home and tells me to call him once I get there. Jacob says he'll be there in a couple of hours once he gets off work. I head over to the home that appears to be in a sketchy part of town.

I arrive at the home and try knocking on the door. No one answers. I call the number Jacob had given me, but there's no answer. By this point, I'm getting a little leery about what's going on. I decide to walk my bike around the block to collect my thoughts.

A guy in his late twenties is walking around and screaming at the top of his lungs to a song that must be blaring in his headphones. Eventually, he walks over to me. He's dripping with sweat and starts talking about how great the water is. He shows me his milk jug filled with water. This dude is *definitely* strung out on something.

Another minute passes and a gang member on a bicycle pulls up next to me. "You want some coke?" He's not asking if I want soda. I sit on the curb, still in my biking outfit, and think, *What the heck is going on?*

About thirty minutes pass. Eventually, my phone rings and it's the guy who runs the house. I talk first. "Hello, Mike. Jacob gave me your number and said you may have a place for me to stay."

"Yeah, man. C'mon over. We're just about to gather for dinner. Come and join us if you'd like."

Because I'm just around the corner, Mike meets me out front. He's in his late fifties but looks like he's ninety. "You can place your bike in the shed behind the house."

I'm not going to lie: I had no idea what I was getting myself into, but I knew God had set this up. All I can do is be obedient.

I ask Mike about the house and its purpose. In a long-winded answer, I gather that this is a house for those coming out of addictions—a recovery house for drug addicts and the homeless.

It's a safe place for those who'd been knocked down, allowing them to get back on their feet. This is a place for those who know their life is a mess and really want to turn it around.

I would learn that the house is fully operated by those who live within it. Mike is the go-to man and facilitator. Each day, they all have chores to accomplish. To stay in the house, they have to pay rent, take frequent drug tests, and attend at least one nightly Bible study each week.

Having to pay for rent and food motivates them to get jobs. It also gives them a hand up rather than a handout.

Mike is a very stern man. His attitude seems to be: "I'm here to help you, but I won't take any of your crap." Still, I think the love he shows these men is exactly what they need. They all know that he'd do anything for them, but he's not going to let them walk all over him. He's had to kick several men out of the home who tried to abuse the system. He hated it but knew it had to be done.

I'd also learn that Mike's life had once been filled with a heavy addiction to meth and alcohol. He'd lost his wife and family due to his addiction. Eventually, he started following Christ and wanted to open a safe home for men in his same situation.

In the recovery home, each of the twelve men had a similar story: extensive abuse, addictions, hang-ups, and problems. Many are divorced or separated from their families due to their problems. One of the housemates is there with his son because they'd do meth together. When I was there, the son was on the streets while the father was in the home. They'd gone out the week prior and lit up together, breaking their probation. Now the son is on the run because he thinks he'll be locked up for life. The father was frantically trying to contact his son and throughout the night he kept confessing his life story to me, trying to seek advice on what to do.

It's beautiful to see these men open up so freely with one another and try to help each other out. That evening, Mike leads a Bible study. Eventually, they allow me to step in and share my experience of the gospel. I get to share several of my stories from the tour and how I've gotten to see Christ move.

I intended to motivate these men to take responsibility for their lives and to push into Christ, but in reality, they motivated me.

Afterward, we all pray together. Later, I have some one-on-ones with a couple of other men who allow me to hear their testimonies.

## Unexpected Acceptance

I was welcomed into a home where the most unlikely people to bring me in brought me in. I had no idea what to expect when I went into the rehab home, but I came out having a completely different outlook on those who struggle and want to change their life.

I always wonder who Jesus would hang out with today. But then I remember that Jesus always had dinner parties with sinners.

# Journal Entry:

# Ears Back

### Day 418

I wish I could fully put into words how I'm feeling about this life-ratifying expedition that is weeks from ending.

I can only describe my particular state of mind through hand gestures and loud grunts. My mind also feels in a state of limbo because I'm not fully convinced that this 440-day voyage is coming to an end. I've become so used to every day being as unpredictable as a toddler's tantrum.

Through the people I've met and the experiences I've had, Bike Through Traffic has completely, extremely, and radically changed my life. Yet, the emotions of heading home and finishing this epic journey are overwhelming.

This expedition put me in situations that were extremely hard to come back from. I struggle to go back to a so-called "normal" lifestyle. But I should have known that my life was never going to be "normal" after my tour.

This is why I'm so torn about being back. I want this to continue, yet I also want there to be a stronger, constant fellowship backing me so I can live the radical lifestyle I've been called to live. If I do something to this extreme again, I'll need someone with me for the whole journey.

We aren't meant to do things alone. Now I know why Jesus sent his disciples out in pairs: if someone is with you who can build you up, then

161

you'll have a much easier time building others up.

The End and the Beginning

My journey back home has me in an "Ears Back" state of mind.

My Grandpa tells a story from his childhood about riding a certain horse that would be sluggish every time they went out for a days ride. The horse didn't want to leave home. But, after going out, as soon as they were heading back to the stable, the horse would pull its ears back and race home.

This is where so many lose focus on their mission and the sole reason why they set out in the first place. Some people think that when climbing a mountain, the end goal is the peak, but it's not. The end goal is arriving back down at the base. Many climbers actually get stuck in terrible situations because they exert all of their energy on the ascent rather than conserving their resources to get them back off the mountain.

We're not finished, until we're finished.

At the same time, so often we look forward to the end rather than being present in the moment. If we're more focused on the finish rather than the journey, we'll miss opportunities. If our focus is in the wrong place, we'll give up before we've even started—or shortly after we've begun.

For all the times I wanted to give up—right before I started, shortly after, and just about every day after that—I'm so glad God let me ride along with Him.


Word out,
Lemke

# Final Ride

*"I believe in Christianity as I believe that the sun has risen: not only because I see it, but because by it I see everything else."*

~ C.S Lewis

Day 438 – Colorado

## Are We There Yet

Coming back home my legs couldn't have peddled any faster. My final week has been a blur, crossing over the Rocky Mountains, sleeping in wide-open fields, church youth rooms, an art studio, and even next to several dinosaur statues.

My last trek before I ride into my hometown where a large crowd of people will be welcoming me back is thrilling. I have to ascend the highest continuous road in America, Trail Ridge Road, peaking at 12,183 feet.

Mike W. (who has been helping me organize my bicycle tour, edit and write my newsletters, and has been setting up my 'Welcome Home' event, just to name a few things he has done) is going to meet me at the base of Trail Ridge and ride over the pass with me.

It is an early morning ride, with a light fog, easy breeze, and roughly 58 degrees. Perfect riding weather.

Mike meets me at the entrance to Rocky Mountain National Park (where the road begins). I catch him and his wife right as they are unloading his bicycle, and we embrace in a long overdue hug.

"You ready for an uphill ride?" Mike says.

"I hope so. I am ready to be home!"

"Do you want to unload your gear into my wife's car?"

"No thank you. I started this tour with it, and I will finish with it."

Little did I know that this ride was going to be one of the most testing rides of my entire tour. It will test my patients, endurance, riding skills, ingenuity, and humility.

## The Ascent
Mike and I start our ride ready to take on the world. The road is long and curvy with rolling hills for the first portion of our ride. Gorgeous evergreen trees and aspens slant up the mountainside and a shallow creek trails alongside the road we are riding along.

I tell Mike stories, as we ride, from the past couple weeks and listen to what is happening in his life. It is refreshing to have someone riding with me. It makes the time pass by ten times quicker.

Roughly ten miles into our ride the road starts its steep ascent towards the peak. All that I am thinking is, *Bring it on. What goes up must come down.*

164

Mike turns to me and says, "Are you going to keep riding after your tour ends?"

"No way. I didn't even like biking before I started this tour. The longest I biked before Bike Through Traffic was maybe twenty miles on a BMX bike. Don't get me wrong; I am glad I did this. The opportunities that came out of this experience I wouldn't change for the world. But I will not be on a tiny seat like this for a very long time."

He chuckles and nods his head.

## The Germans

Mike and I have ascended nearly 2,000 feet in elevation. The temperature has dropped to 42 degrees and a consistent rain has started. The road is very steep making us travel at a max speed of four miles per hour. My legs are spinning quickly but each revolution seems to only move me an inch at a time.

After five hours of cycling we reach the peak. We gawk at our total elevation gain of 4,314 feet. This is my second highest climb of the tour (first being 7,621 feet traveling from Salt Lake City, UT to Strawberry Reservoir in Utah).

The rain by this point is coming down in buckets. Due to the lack of trees this high Mike and I find refuge in the welcome center at the top.

There is a very large crowd of people all huddled together trying to dry off and get warm. A German family who took interest in my bicycle greets Mike and me. They offer to buy us some hot chocolate in exchange for some stories. We take a seat at a long table with a large window in front of us that overlooks the valley below. After asking them their story, I dive right into many stories explaining that I have just completed fifteen months of touring raising awareness about domestic sex trafficking.

The German couple introduces me to their daughter who is attending university in America and is part of a group at her school that is working on a fundraiser and awareness event for sex trafficking. I was able to give her some information and help her brainstorm some ideas she could use.

## The Tourist

A little less than two hours have passed and the rain has cleared. We say our goodbyes and the two of us, still wet, get back on our bikes ready to ride the steep mountain road down into Estes Park, CO.

A thick fog envelops the tundra making it hard to see more than ten feet in front of us. Having a heavy loaded bike helps to propel me down the mountain. Also having highly warned down break pads from the thousands of miles of riding makes it much harder to slow down.

The road looks open and free for me to ride at a heightened pace. I was wrong.

No more than a mile into my decent I see a faint object quickly approaching me. Well, actually, I was quickly approaching it. Lucky for me, my quick reflexes jolt me out of my lane into the oncoming traffic due to a Texas suburban stopped smack-dab in the middle of the two-lane road with no shoulders or rails, and a steep drop-off into the valley.

Thinking to myself, *Only a Texan*, while checking my six to see if Mike got around the inconvenient tourist, I give off a sigh of relief for avoiding a potentially dangerous situation.

As my head pivots back around front I realize my reflexes could never of been fast enough. The descending road still continues to curve; I however, do not curve with it.

The turn of events that take place all seem to happen in slow motion. As my bike Sophia and I cling onto one another while being projected off the side of the cliff like a slingshot, about seven different thoughts run through my head. None of which are remotely appropriate to repeat except for one; *I'm flying Jack!*

Next thing I know I am wrapped around my bicycle like tangled headphones with my gear flung fifteen feet all around me. Mike saw the whole thing and comes to my aid as the tourist drives by like nothing happened.

With laughter in my voice I simply say, "Ouch."

I gather my bike: bent handlebars and broken front brake. I place my gear back on Sophia. Thankfully all that happened to me was a mildly scratched leg that made me limp for only a short bit.

As I descend Trail Ridge Road, I couldn't help but laugh thinking; *I have gone 12,000+ miles not wrecking once. Then I get within a stone throw away from home and crash.*

It only took me thirty-eight minutes to ride into Estes Park from the peak of Trail Ridge. As I enter my familiar hometown I let out many loud screams of pure joy.

My closest friends, Caleb, Aishlinn, and Elijah are waiting for me in town. It is as if I had never left them.

## Welcome Home Daniel

I spend the night in Estes Park. On July 2, 2016 I am greeted by twenty friends who want to ride the final stretch with me from Estes

Park to Loveland, CO. Among them is the cofounder of RestoreOne, Chris Smith, my older brother Vince, best friend Elijah, some pastors from church, and my Texas friends Jana and Charise.

The plan is to ride into Loveland, do some interviews with TV and Newspaper companies, and than ride over to the church for the welcome home event Mike set up. The day couldn't have gone anymore perfectly.

With the American flag in my hand and my bicycle in the other, I turn the corner to the street I grew up on (and the starting point for this tour) I hear my mom yelling, "Yeh-haa!" I see a giant yellow sign she made saying, "Welcome Home Daniel".

## Sparrow in the Crowd

My church has a Saturday service preceding the welcome home party. Pastor Tim invited me to speak during service about my tour as well as Chris and Anna Smith from RestoreOne.

During that time we invited the church congregation to join us afterwards for food, and live music.

During the event I was frantically trying to hug everyone at the party while trying to realize that my tour was over. Once things seemed to settle down a man walked up to me. Sean Wheeler shared with me his story.

I won't call him a victim or a survivor because that isn't what he calls himself. He simply says, "I am a thriver".

Sean wheeler spent his early years growing up in Iowa and by the time he was five years old, he was taken to a shed in a backyard and raped for the first time.

From that time until he was nine years old, the older boy from the shed would find him and repeat the molestations.

168

Sean says: "Early on I fought back for a brief time, as much as a little kid can. Till one day in the back of a house I found myself with 3 older guys, probably college age. I struggled against them and the ringleader finally told his friends to stretch me out, he wanted me to feel it. They grabbed me by the hands and feet, and pulled me tight. He then hit my backside and pretty much beat the fight out me. When they let go of my limbs I went numb inside and silent, till just a few years ago."

Sean was between 5 and 6 years old at the time and in later years other predators would hit him again after they were done sexually abusing the boy.

He only remembers one time where it was one guy. Every time after that it was two to four guys.

By the time he was seven, a woman led him to a house where he was used in pornography with another boy and a girl, and two men. .

Even though Sean would eventually go home after each instance his parents never knew. He still attended church, went to school, and sung in choir. His mother instilled in him how to pray and made sure that they prayed often.

When he was 9 years old Sean's family moved away from that town in Iowa and the predatory abuse stopped. Still, he was by then caught in a trap that he says he didn't even know existed. His self-image was set as somehow being deserving of that behavior from others, and not having any value to people or God. It would set him on a pattern of destructive self-behavior for decades, combined with a desperate sadness inside that he says he could not understand.

Not knowing it was a trigger word for Sean, I asked him, "How old are you?" With a polite and calm voice, but a remembrance in his eyes, he tells me, "That phrase used to scare me." There were a few times he was hurt for not being the "right age". As a coping mechanism he learned to lie about it, his age, and saying it out loud still makes him uncomfortable and wonder what people are expecting when they ask that question, who ever they are even now. After a while he stopped celebrating his birthday because in Sean's eyes he was just a 'thing', and why should a thing ever be celebrated.

He sees all of the anti sex trafficking organizations that promote the idea that the only people being abused are girls and women, with men being the lone predators. Most predators are male but not all. He also sees that these organizations say that the average age is 12-14. When I asked him what his thoughts were on this he said, "It makes my heart hurt knowing that nearly half of sexual abuse cases are boys and men, and they are not being talked about. He doesn't accept the average age statistic either, as he knows that for both girls and boys it can be much younger."

Sean's story is powerful. As I am listening to his testimony while hundreds of people are walking around, I feel as if it is just he and I alone. I eventually ask him to tell me how he got to where he is now.

## Reintegration

Sean goes on telling me his testimony, "I remember the last time the molestation happened in Iowa. I hid in my closet and wept. As I was in there I prayed to God asking for His help. In that moment God gave me a peace, and I stopped crying. God answered my prayer because after that we moved to a different state and no one from that group ever touched me again."

Eventually Sean would join the Navy and become an officer. He attended the University of Kansas getting a bachelor in journalism and later earned a master's in landscape architecture in Colorado.

While in the Navy, Sean would find himself standing outside a church just listening to the music. Every time someone would try and talk to him he would decline the invitation thinking, *I am trespassing in Gods house. I'm not good enough to be in there.*

Luckily a lady at work wanted to get to know Sean more deeply. Eventually they started dating but he never seemed to open up to her fully. Years of trauma and PTSD were still taking place. One day she brings this up to Sean and asks him why he is so distant.

He told her, "People did things to me when I was little. I am damaged goods. How could you possibly want me?"

Sean says today, "I thought there, it's out. If you want to leave you can and at least you'll know it is not your fault". This incredible woman looked at him and said, "I love you and I don't care."

That night with her was the first time Sean had ever shared his story of being trafficked with anyone. A year later he marries her.

By 2011 Sean had found his way back inside of a church and was at a service where the main speaker was a counselor for trauma. After her talk Sean meets with her and tried to stumble his way through an introduction to her. The first words out of her mouth were, "So when were you abuse?"

Sean breaks down crying and asks, "How did you know?"

"I can see it in your eyes." She told him.

After that she began counseling with Sean.

On May 26, 2011 his counselor with the help of another powerful woman of prayer helped release twelve demons from Sean! The next morning Sean's wife said, "That was the first time I have ever seen you sleep in peace."

Later Sean would go into prison ministry to help predators. When

I asked why, he said he had the same question for the Holy Spirit. The answer he got from the Spirit was, "I am sending you there because you know how they think."

A man who was imprisoned for child pornography was talking with Sean during his time in a prison, "How can a man like you forgive a man like me?"

"Because God forgave me. You go find forgiveness at the cross." Sean tells me that you could see a weight fall off this man.

His counselor would advise him to write his thoughts down because God has given him a voice. Now Sean Wheeler is a published author, and you can read his book titled, "Wretch".

At the end Sean simply said to me, "The ringleader is now dead, but I pray that he was saved. It was easier for me to forgive them for what they did to me, after I had forgiven myself. I kept blaming myself thinking 'I let them do it'. Not realizing it was not my fault."

Sean's story was an answer to prayer for me. I had been debating what to do after Bike Through Traffic, but he made it very clear. I need to help Sparrows reintegrate back into society so that they can live the life they deserve. I need to help them find jobs.

Sean came from a background of trauma, but is living a life of peace and forgiveness. He is thriving.

*Daniel arriving back home to Colorado July 2, 2016*

# Life after the Saddle

*"Deep down you may still be that same great kid you used to be. But it's not who you are underneath, it's what you do that defines you."*

~ Rachel Dawes

What's next? Where does one go after traveling the United States for fifteen months on a bicycle and having gotten used to the life on the road?

Well, I have a couple of options. I could just go back to my everyday life, live with what I've learned, and ignore the problem, convincing myself that I've done enough to help. Or I could continue to step out in blind faith and walk through the door Christ has opened for me.

But the last time I walked through a door like that, it forced me to fully put my trust in something other than myself. It was by far the most tested I've ever been and the most faith-stretching experience I've ever been exposed to.

I always tell people who are not Christians or are struggling with their faith to step outside of their comfort zone—to really test themselves and go against what society tells them to do because that's when Christ shows up in crazy awesome ways.

As I keep moving forward, I'm choosing to rely on Jesus rather than myself. With that, some pretty amazing doors have flung open.

When I cycled through central California, I met an old friend of mine. Actually, he was my very first camp counselor at Covenant Heights, Greg. Now, he's the head pastor at Cornerstone Covenant. While in California, we spoke for a while about what's next for me. I talked about how I want to start a nonprofit business that hires survivors of sex trafficking after they've gone through a recovery program. I want to reintegrate them back into society and teach them basic job skills so they can thrive in society as a "normal" human being.

With all that alone time on the road, I've thought a lot about many different jobs that would be helpful and educating, yet not overwhelming for a Sparrow. Many ideas have crossed my path, but the best one I'm going after is, well, a little different.

## Aquaponics: The Next Dream

Aquaponics is urban farming that combines aquaculture (raising fish) and hydroponics (the soilless growing of plants) to grow fish and plants together in one integrated system. Fish waste provides an organic food source for the growing plants and the plants provide a natural filter for the water that the fish live in. In other words, it's a cycling ecosystem to grow plants and vegetables without the requirement of land to plant crops in.

I'm choosing an aquaponics farm, because running one is relatively stress-free and educational. It teaches the Sparrows basic job skills like coming to work, cleaning up their designated area, taking care of a product, agriculture, and watching their progress from start to finish. They'll work with the same people and won't have the stress of customers. It can be easy work because the Sparrows will cut plants and reseed, but it can be complicated and technical because of the chemistry and biology needed to know in order to operate the system.

My philosophy on the greenhouse is to build it so well initially, that we won't have to keep rebuilding. Also, if the facility looks good and is well taken care of, the Sparrows are going to find more worth in their work and feel more respected. I'd like to have three to six four-thousand-square-foot greenhouses in order to keep up with productivity. Also, if one facility is down for maintenance, we'll be able to use the others to keep up with production.

As for the produce we grow, we will sell the product at Farmers Markets. We will sell to local restaurants that market themselves as a farm-to-table, organic restaurant—not to mention the moral boost they get from helping those in need. Eventually we will start up our own restaurant that hires Sparrows.

This will offer a sort of graduation system that teaches the Sparrows a new set of job skills. At such a restaurant, Sparrows work with customers, effectively "build" a product, and work with cash flow. This establishment adds a faster pace to the professional educational system.

With counsel from my Board Members, and other friends, we concluded that a cafe/sandwich shop would be best. First off, sandwiches are the bomb. Secondly, a cafe would use a wide variety of vegetables from the aquaponics farm. Once again, an ecosystem exists within the businesses as well.

There will be a bakery within the cafe, which lowers the cost of bread and teaches the Sparrows yet another job skill. We will locally source meat and cheese, too, making this the best farm-to-table cafe in the world.

These two businesses sustain each other and give people the ability to get back on their feet.

Statistically, 86 percent of victims who are brought out of sex trafficking and are not placed in a helpful program, go back into it. Our hope is to put a huge dent in this figure. We want to set in motion a hand up, rather than a handout, for these men and women. We want to give them basic skills they can use when applying for other jobs, that don't involve soliciting their bodies to make a living. [16]

A job application program will exist to provide us with the option to choose the Sparrows whom we think would work best together. We'll partner with safe houses across the country and set up a rapport with the survivors who are going through a rehab program so that they feel safe when they come to our reintegration program.

We'll also set an end date for each person who comes through our program based on his or her specific needs to ensure they're as prepared as possible for future jobs.

The purpose of all this is to educate and reintegrate the Sparrow, giving them applicable job skills that will help further their success down the road of life. This program is not meant to be a career for them, but rather a stepping-stone toward a new life.

Hopefully, if everything goes according to plan, we will be under the new organization name, *Bold Love Foundation.*

## Bold Love Foundation

All the puzzle pieces fit together in California. Greg has been dreaming about starting an aquaponics farm as well and using its proceeds to help missionaries. On top of that, an entrepreneurial member of his congregation named Mark also wants to start a nursery. Greg scheduled a meeting for us all to discuss the possibility of joining together.

After talking for a couple of hours and throwing around many great ideas, Mark offered his private airport, on which to build our aquaponics farm! It's on the outskirts of town, which allows the Sparrows not to feel as if they're being watched all the time, and this solution is much cheaper than buying our own property.

Basically, I see dominoes all lined up in a beautifully intricate pattern and the first couple of dominoes have been knocked down.

## Still Biking Through Traffic

What's going to happen to Bike Through Traffic? I've put a lot of thought into this as well. There are organizations that set up coast-to-coast bicycle tours to raise awareness about their causes, as well as for service projects and fundraising. They get fifteen to thirty riders that each raise a certain amount of money to ride. They get a support van that follows them with all their gear and they sleep in churches, YMCAs, and campgrounds.

I want to take this concept to help raise awareness about domestic sex trafficking. I want to do what I did on the Bike Through Traffic tour but with a large group of people.

For me, I found that nailing down a place to sleep was the most difficult and stressful part of my entire tour. I contemplated how I could bring the house with us. Then I remembered the tiny house movement. I thought, "What if I converted a school bus into a home?"

I did some research and found that I could get a school bus and fit twenty-one beds inside. They'd be bunk beds, stacked three high, with a bathroom in the bus as well. We would have a stove that pulls out from underneath the bus for all the cooking, and if we could get a sponsorship, we would run the electronics on solar power. Otherwise, we'd use propane.

The tour would start on the West coast and go to the East coast—it's a much easier ride that way. It would take two months and along the way we'd speak at churches and have fundraising events set up.

To help cut down on costs, we'd try to get local churches to donate food to us: oatmeal, noodles, rice, chicken, eggs, power bars, honey, power food, etc. If we're cooking our own food, each person should cost ten dollars per day, at most. We can cut that number drastically if we plan right.

I also think about how my solo reach on social media was pretty extensive, and I can't help but think about having twenty-one *other* people and their social media reach. That could be a very large outreach.

If this plan works, Bike Through Traffic would fundraise for the reintegration program to help survivors get jobs.

It will be a life-changing experience for those whom you ride for.

The money and the effort are for the least of these.

## How can you help?

First and foremost is prayer. Everything and anything we do from here on out needs to be covered in prayer, because if it isn't Christ's plan, then it isn't our plan.

Second, help us make connections. If you know anyone who you think would want to help with this, please get them in contact with us. Tell your friends and get them involved. Talk to them about this book and help spread the word. Help me get this book in places and to people I could not.

Lastly, money is a necessity. Obviously, this will be a big and ongoing endeavor, but I think my track record shows that when I put my mind to something, I get it done.

If you'd like to donate, visit our website:
www.BikeThruTraffic.com/donate

Remember, together we can break the cycle.

Your support is your first step to Kissing Lions.

Visit our website (if it hasn't been hacked again!) at:
www.BikeThruTraffic.com

www.BoldLoveFoundation.com

**Instagram:**     @BikeThroughTraffic

@BoldLoveFoundation

Watch some of Bike Through Traffics videos:
YouTube.com/BikeThroughTraffic

Facebook.com/BikeThroughTraffic

# Appendix 1:

# How You Can Fight Sex Trafficking

*"A study by The John Jay College and the Center for Court Innovation estimated that, in 2008, as high as 50% of the commercially sexually exploited (CSE) children in the United States were boys."*
~ RestoreOne

Where does one even begin to fight against sex trafficking? How does someone determine who is legitimately a slave versus someone who actually wants to do it for themselves? How do you find a person who started off as a slave and then has been so brainwashed that they believe it's perfectly okay for them to be sold for sex?

## Look for visible indicators of trafficking at commercial establishments:

•      Do you see heavy security, locked doors, electronic surveillance, or barred windows?

•      Is the place in an isolated location?

- How much foot traffic goes into and out of the location?

- Are employees allowed to leave the site? Or are they never seen leaving the grounds other than with a personal escort? Are they driven to and from the premises by a guard? Some slaves aren't allowed to leave. They're imprisoned at the location. Some victims are even kept under surveillance when taken to the doctor, hospital, or clinic for treatment. The trafficker may act as a translator or boyfriend.

- How does an employee act, especially when alone? If the victim is allowed to leave by him or herself and isn't escorted anywhere by his or her pimp, you must look at the way they're acting.

- Are there any markings on their body, like a tattoo or branding? Tattoos of names, or even ones that say Daddy, can be an indicator. Often, pimps will have their slaves call them Daddy to imprint their fatherly role onto their victim. It's part of the brainwashing.

It's not always easy to see these signs because the evidence could be circumstantial.

We also need to remember that slaves are kept in bondage through a combination of fear, intimidation, abuse, betrayal of their basic human rights, and psychological control by their trafficker. This kind of slavery doesn't mean that they're physically locked up in chains. Most of the time, they're enslaved by psychological manipulation. Each victim will have different experiences, but they all share a common thread that may signify a life of indentured servitude.

## Look for the signs of a sex-trafficked victim:

- Since the trafficked individual may be treated as a disposable possession, health problems may abound, e.g., malnutrition, dehydration, poor personal hygiene, sexually transmitted diseases, signs of rape or sexual abuse, bruising, broken bones, critical illnesses like diabetes, cancer, or heart disease, and/or signs of untreated medical problems.

- The victim may not hold his or her identity or travel documents.

- The person they're with could also be an indicator. The trafficker may have a lot of money on them while the victim has little to none.

- The victim may be quiet. Most victims aren't going to voluntarily release information about their enslavement because they're afraid of what their trafficker will do. Even if continuously pressed, they may not budge for fear of their lives as well as the lives of their family.

How can you approach such a situation without blowing their cover or getting them into trouble with their trafficker? How can you talk to them in a way that won't harm either party? Know this first: when questioning victims, approach the situation with extreme caution. If you say or do something wrong, you could endanger not only the victim's life, but you could put yourself in harm's way too. Sex traffickers see themselves as inventory managers, and if you mess up their inventory, they may want to likewise mess you up. I strongly advise you to asses the situation and possibly call the police before addressing the situation. Never approach a victim without being trained. With that said, consider using these questions, but do so cautiously and with much prayer:

- "Are you free to leave work and come talk with me?"

This gets them away and lets you know better if they're a prisoner or not, but their ability to leave doesn't always verify if they're being trafficked.

- "Do you have a valid ID on you?"

This lets you know if they're being kept at their "job" because they can't travel, which is a form of enslavement.

• "What's your pay? What's it like working there? What are the conditions of your employment?"

This allows you to understand if they're getting paid fairly or if they're a part of the labor trafficking industry, if not the sex trafficking industry.

• "What's your living situation like? Do you live at home or near where you work?"

This could tell you about a portion of their life and freedom outside of their work.

• "How'd you get your job?" or, if they seem to be from another country, "What brought you to the States?"

I think these are the most important questions you could ask as their answer may help you better assess what their work is actually all about.

I believe it's important to question as many people as possible, even if it's only a small percent, so that we'll be able to get them out of the terrible situations they're in. I'd much rather question someone who's doing it because he or she wants to and let them do their thing rather than not question a person and later find out they were a trafficked victim and I didn't do anything to help.[17]

## To Make a Difference

The fight to end sex trafficking involves every state coming together and cracking down on this epidemic taking over America. Sending letters to our representatives and governors could help out a lot, but only if we expose the issue to everyone and not let it become yet another issue swept under the rug. I believe we can really make a difference, not only for our nation, but also for the victims directly affected by sex trafficking.

Sex trafficking is no small feat to take on. We need a lot of training and the help, as well as knowledge, of those who have already been in the fight for a long time. We need to remember that we are one body and when one of us is hurting, all of us are hurting. Just like the hand needs the arm and the foot needs the leg, these victims need our help. One can't function without the other.

Not all of us can go out and head into this fight and we can't all get personal experience with the victims themselves, but we all can help in some way: through donations to worthy causes, spreading information on social media, or talking about the epidemic and its cure at social gatherings. If someone brings it up, then it will make people think about its horrors and want to change it. We need to stop living in a culture of naiveté that doesn't want to admit there's a problem.

As I like to put it, "Make it famous and people will listen." Even if it's only for a day that people talk about it, then at least the issue is exposed and people will better recognize it once they see it—and possibly do something about it. But most people aren't even aware that sex trafficking is happening in their towns and cities because it doesn't directly affect them.

Last, yet most important, is prayer. Jesus is our commander and chief. He is leading this battle and it is our duty to talk with Him and let Him lead us.

I love the story of the little boy walking along the shoreline of a beach who sees that thousands of starfish have washed up on the sand. He bends down and throws one back into the ocean, finds another and throws it back, then finds one more and throws it back into the ocean.

An old man sees him do this over and over, so he stops the boy and says, "But there must be tens of thousands of starfish on this beach. I'm afraid you won't really be able to make much of a difference."

The little boy looks up at him with a starfish in his hand, looks at the starfish, looks back at the old man, and throws the starfish back in the ocean. Simply, he says, "It made a difference to that one!" [18]

The only problem with that story is that there's only one person on the shore, frantically trying to save the starfish.

When we work together as the body of Christ, we can eradicate sex trafficking.

# Appendix 2:
# Tour Stats

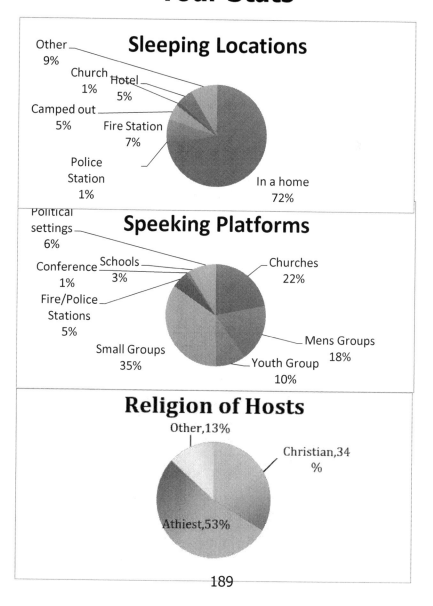

**Sleeping Locations**

Other 9%
Church 1%
Hotel 5%
Camped out 5%
Fire Station 7%
Police Station 1%
In a home 72%

**Speeking Platforms**

Political settings 6%
Conference 1%
Schools 3%
Fire/Police Stations 5%
Small Groups 35%
Youth Group 10%
Mens Groups 18%
Churches 22%

**Religion of Hosts**

Other,13%
Christian,34%
Athiest,53%

| | |
|---:|:---|
| **Miles Traveled:** | 12,607.97 |
| **Days on the road:** | 440 days (15 months) |
| **Average miles a day:** | 55.9 miles |
| **Number of states:** | 37 States plus Ontario Province, Canada |
| **Number of Countries:** | 2 |
| **Number of dog chases:** | 89 |
| **Sets of Tires:** | 3 |
| **Number of tubes:** | 30 |
| **Estimated total calories burned:** | 719,759 |
| **Total elevation gain:** | 325,049 Feet |
| **Total time in the saddle:** | 1,066:48 hours |
| **Starting body weight:** | 191 lbs. |
| **Ending body weight:** | 167 lbs. |
| **Number of Crashes:** | 1 |
| **Estimated fluid intake:** | 605 gallons or 77,440oz |
| | |
| **Replacement parts:** | 4 chains<br>3 spokes<br>1 rear rim<br>2 brake pads<br>3 bottom brackets<br>1 crank set<br>1 cassette<br>1 rear rack<br>2 gloves<br>2 handlebar wraps |
| | |
| **Average daily spending:** | $4.80 |
| **Nights slept outside:** | 21 |
| **Bear encounters:** | 2 |
| **Alligator encounters:** | 4 |

## Clothes

4 bike shorts
4 boxers
3 running shorts
2 bike jerseys
4 t-shirts
2 tank tops
1 pair of leggings

5 socks
1 blue jeans
1 light jacket
1 dress shirt
1 rain jacket
1 down jacket (doubled as pillow)

2 gloves (cycling and winter)
1 beanie
1 belt
1 Buff
Chaco's
Mountain cycling shoes

## Toiletries

Deodorant
Powdered Toothpaste
Toothbrush
Electronic shaver

Beard oil
Microfiber towel
Contact case and solution

Natural muscle cream
Aloe Vera
Glasses and contacts

## Bags

1 Jandd handlebar bag
2 Ortleib back panniers

1 Large dry sack

3 large vacuum seal bags

## Camping

1 tent (Big Agnes Angel Spring UL2)
1 Eno Hammock
1 Pocket Rocket camp stove w/ propane

2 lighters
Cutlery set
Clif Bars (Varied)
2 water bottles (21 oz)
1 sleeping bag (Marmot 50 Rampart down)

1 Nalgene (64 oz)

Tubular webbing
Paracord

## Electronics

Cell phone
Multi-USB charger

Ipod
Ipad

GoPro
Garmin 810

## Bike
2013 Specialized AWOL
Rear bike rack
Helmet
Combo bike lock

## Tools/ Emergency kits
4 bike tubes
1 extra tire
Vitamin C
Ultima (Electrolyte powder)
1 muscle roller
Chain lube

## First Aid Kit
Super glue
Matches
Ibuprofen
Sting and bite pads
2 wraps
Sports tape
Sunscreen
Gauze pads
Vitamin C
Ibuprofen

# Bike Through Traffic Tour

## Sunday April 19 2015
Longmont, CO
Denver, CO
Colorado Springs, CO
Hugo/Kaval, CO
Kit Carson, CO
Lamar, CO
Syracuse, CO
Holcomb, KS
Dodge City, KS
Pratt, KS
Argonia, KS
Ponca, KS

## May 2015
Pawhuska, OK
Tulsa, OK
Chouteau, OK
Colcord, OK
Fayetteville, AR
Bella Vista, AR
Joplin, MO
Fort Scott, KS
Wellsville, KS
Lawrence, KS
Kansas City, MO
Warrensburg, MO

## June 2015
Boonville, MO
Jefferson City, MO
Washington, MO
St. Louis, MO
New Douglas, IL
Springfield, IL

## June 2015 (Cont.)
Normal, IL
Dwight, IL
Joliet, IL
Chicago, IL
Portage, IN
Sawyer, MI
South Haven, MI
Wyoming, MI
St Johns, MI
Flushing, MI
Lapeer, MI
Marine City, MI
Strathroy, ON
London, ON

## July 2015
Brantford, ON
St Catharines, ON
Sanborn, NY
Albion, NY
Rochester, NY
Clifton Springs, NY
Baldwinsville, NY
Watertown, NY
Canton, NY
Malone, NY
Plattsburgh, NY
Burlington, VT
Montpelier, VT
Lancaster, NH
Gorham, NH
Wilton, ME
Unity, ME

## July 2015 (Cont.)
Bangor, ME
Waterville, ME
Lisbon, ME
Portland, ME
Portsmouth, NH
Boston, MA
Providence, RI
Windham, CT
Hartford, CT
New haven, CT

## August 2015
Stamford, CT
Manhattan, NY
New York, NY
Long Island, NY
Newark, NJ
Trenton, NJ
Philadelphia, PA
Atlantic City, NJ
Cape May, NJ
Dover, DE
Port Deposit, MD
Baltimore, MD
Washington D.C
Gainesville, VA
Fredericksburg, VA
Richmond, VA
Williamsburg, VA
Suffolk, VA
Virginia Beach, VA
Suffolk, VA
Sussex, VA
Petersburg, VA

## September 2015

Farmville, VA
Lynchburg, VA
South Boston, VA
Raleigh, NC
Greenville, NC
Jacksonville, NC
Wilmington, NC
South Brunswick NC
Myrtle Beach, SC

Georgetown, SC
Charleston, SC
Beaufort, SC
Savannah, GA
Darien, GA
Kingsland, GA
Jacksonville, FL
St Augustine, FL
Daytona Beach, FL
Port St John, FL

## October, 2015

Vero Beach FL
Jupiter, FL
Boca Raton, FL
Miami, FL
Midway Campground
Naples, FL
Cape Coral, FL

Punta Gorda, FL
Sarasota, FL

Tampa, FL
Spring Hill, FL
Crystal River FL
Fanning Springs, FL
Spring Hill, FL
Crystal River FL

Fanning Springs, FL

Perry, FL
Tallahassee, FL
Albany, GA
Butler GA
Griffin, GA
Barnesville, GA
Atlanta, GA
LaGrange, GA
Auburn, AL

## November 2015

Montgomery, AL
Selma, AL
Demopolis, AL
Meridian, MS
Newton, MS
Jackson, MS
Mendenhall, MS
Prentiss, MS
Bogalusa, LA
Slidell, LA
New Orleans, LA
Baton Rouge, LA

Opelousas, LA
Le Blanc, LA
Beaumont, TX
Kingwood, TX
Houston, TX
Katy, TX

## December 2015

Woodlands, TX
Columbus, TX
Shinner, TX
San Antonio, TX
Buda, TX
Georgetown, TX
Taylor, TX

Temple, TX
Waco, TX

## December 2015 (Cont.)

Waxahachie, TX
Dallas, TX
Anna, TX
Copper Canyon
Weatherford, TX
Ranger, TX
Abilene, TX

## January 2016

Sweetwater, TX
Snyder, TX
Post, TX
Lubbock, TX
Brownfield, TX
Hobbs, NM
Carlsbad, NM
Guadalupe Mtns, TX
El Paso, TX
Las Cruces, NM
Deming, NM
Lordsburg, NM
San Simon, AZ

Willcox, AZ
Benson, AZ
Tucson, AZ
Arizona City, AZ
Phoenix, AZ

## February, 2016

Gila Bend, AZ
Tacna, AZ

Yuma, AZ
El Centro, CA
Alpine, CA
San Diego, CA

## March, 2016

San Clemente, CA
Los Angeles, CA
Malibu, CA

## April 2016

Santa Barbara, CA
Santa Maria, CA
San Simeon CA
Big Sur CA
Hollister, CA
Turlock, CA
Hilmar CA
Fairfield, CA
Lodi, CA
Sacramento CA
Chico, CA
Redding, CA

## May 2016

Mount Shasta, CA
Yreka, CA
Medford, OR
Myrtle Creek, OR
Cottage Grove, OR
Corvallis OR
Salem, OR
Portland, OR
Longview, WA
Olympia, WA
Seattle, WA
Snoqualmie Pass, WA
Ellensburg, WA
Othello, WA
Washtucna, WA
Pomeroy, WA
Clarkson, WA
Grangeville, ID

## June 2016

Missoula, MT
Drummond, MT
Butte, MT
Three Forks, MT
Bozeman, MT
West Yellowstone, MT
Ashton, ID
Idaho Falls, ID
Pocatello, ID
Preston, ID
Logan, UT
Salt Lake City, UT
Daniel Summit
Roosevelt, UT
Dinosaur, CO
Craig, CO
Steamboat, CO
Grandby, CO
Estes Park, CO

## July 2, 2016

Loveland, CO

195

# References

[1] Keesey, B. (n.d.). Our Story. November, 2004 https://invisiblechildren.com/our-story/

[2] Federation for American Immigration Reform's "Human Trafficking—Exploitation of Illegal Aliens," August 2005 http://www.fairus.org/issue/human-trafficking-exploitation-of-illegal-aliens

[3] Homeland Security. Human Trafficking. November 07, 2016. http://www.dhs.gov/topic/human-trafficking

[4] McBane, D. (2014, April 07). The Facts: What is Sex Trafficking and How Widespread Is It? *Focus on the Family*. http://www.focusonthefamily.com/socialissues/family/sex-trafficking/sex-trafficking-the-facts

[5] "Sex Trafficking," *Polaris Project*, https://polarisproject.org/sex-trafficking.

[6] Bureau of Public Affairs. "U.S. Laws on Trafficking in Person." *U.S. Department of State*, U.S. Department of State, www.state.gov/j/tip/laws/

[7] O'Neill Richard, Amy. "International Trafficking in Women to the United States: A Contemporary Manifestation of Slavery and Organized Crime." Center for the Study of Intelligence, Nov. 1999, www.cia.gov/library/center-for-the-study-of-intelligence/csi-publications/books-and-monographs/trafficking.pdf

[8] Walker-Rodriquez, Amanda, and Rodney Hill. "Human Sex Trafficking." FBI, 1 Mar. 2011, www.leb.fbi.gov/articles/featured-articles/human-sex-trafficking

[9] Karin Lehnardt, "56 Little Known Facts about Human Trafficking," *Fact Retriever*, September 20, 2016, https://www.factretriever.com/human-trafficking-facts.

[10] Nathan Harden, "Eight Facts You Didn't Know About Child Sex Trafficking," *Huffington Post*, November 11, 2013, http://www.huffingtonpost.com/nathan-harden/eight-facts-you-didnt-know_b_4221632.html.

[11] Bo Rader, "Dodge City woman sentenced to 21 years for child porn," *The Wichita Eagle*, July 18, 2016, http://www.kansas.com/news/local/crime/article90382042.html.

[12] Jessica Reichert and Amy Sylwestrzak, "National Survey of Residential Programs for Victims of Sex Trafficking," The Illinois Criminal Justice Information Authority, October 2013, http://www.icjia.state.il.us/assets/pdf/ResearchReports/NSRHVST_101813.pdf, p. 12

[13] Shultz, David. "Divorce rates double when people start watching porn." Science Mag, 26 Aug. 2016, www.sciencemag.org/news/2016/08/divorce-rates-double-when-people-start-watching-porn.

[14] Matt Chandler, "Exodus (Part 5) — Sojourner," September 18, 2016, transcript, The Village Church, Flower Mound, TX, http://media.thevillagechurch.net/sermons/transcripts/201609180900FMWC21ASAAA _MattChandler_ExodusPt5- Sojourner.pdf.

[15] Derek Sivers, "First Follower: Leadership Lessons from a Dancing Guy," February

11, 2010, https://sivers.org/ff.

[16] Johnson, Debbie. "Our Impact." Without Permission, withoutpermission.org/

[17] Smith, Linda. "Demanding Justice." Shared Hope, 2014, sharedhope.org/wp-content/uploads/2014/08/Demanding_Justice_Report_2014.pdf.

[18] Peter Straube, "The Starfish Story: one step towards changing the world," *EventsForChange*, June 5, 2011, https://eventsforchange.wordpress.com/2011/06/05/the-starfish-story-one-step-towards-changing-the-world/.

DOJ, Assessment of U.S. Government Activities to Combat Trafficking in Persons: September 2007

GAO, Human Trafficking: A Strategic Framework Could Help Enhance the Interagency

Collaboration Needed to Effectively Combat Trafficking Crimes: 2007.

"Policy Development." *Shared Hope International.* N.p., n.d. Web. 07 Dec. 2013.

"Safe Houses for Victims of Trafficking Remains an Urgent Need." *Dominican Sisters of Peace.* N.p., n.d. Web. 04 Dec. 2013. http://www.oppeace.org/node/5915

"Hostess/Strip Clubs - Sex Trafficking | Polaris Project | Combating Human Trafficking and Modern-day Slavery." *Hostess/Strip Clubs - Sex Trafficking | Polaris Project | Combating Human Trafficking and Modern-day Slavery.* N.p., n.d. Web. 19 Nov. 2013.

Harden, Nathan. "Eight Facts You Didn't Know About Child Sex Trafficking." *The Huffington Post.* TheHuffingtonPost.com, 11 Nov. 2013. Web. 20 Nov. 2013.

US State Department, Trafficking in Persons Report (2007) p.36

Jazmine Ulloa, "*Sex Traffickers Prove Harder to Catch as They Move Online.*" Austin News, Sports, Weather, Longhorns, Business. N.p., n.d. Web. 01 Dec. 2013.

60901515R00111

Made in the USA
San Bernardino, CA
13 December 2017